Sports Fundamentals Series

BOWLING
Fundamentals

Michelle Mullen

Human Kinetics

Library of Congress Cataloging-in-Publication Data

Human Kinetics Publishers.
  Bowling fundamentals / Human Kinetics with Michelle Mullen
        p.   cm.
    ISBN 0-7360-5120-1
  1. Bowling.   I. Mullen, Michelle.   II. Title.
  GV903 .B69   2004
  794.6--dc21

                                                                    2003013368

ISBN: 0-7360-5120-1

Acquisitions Editor: Dean Miller; **Developmental Editor:** Cynthia McEntire; **Assistant Editor:** Scott Hawkins; **Copyeditor:** Jan Feeney; **Proofreader:** Jennifer L. Davis; **Graphic Designer:** Robert Reuther; **Graphic Artist:** Tara Welsch; **Photo and Art Manager:** Dan Wendt; **Cover Designer:** Keith Blomberg; **Photographer (cover):** Dan Wendt; **Photographer (interior):** Tom Roberts; **Illustrator:** Brian McElwain; **Printer:** United Graphics

Human Kinetics books are available at special discounts for bulk purchase. Special editions or book excerpts can also be created to specification. For details, contact the Special Sales Manager at Human Kinetics.

Printed in the United States of America   10 9 8 7 6 5 4 3 2

Human Kinetics
Web site: www.HumanKinetics.com

United States: Human Kinetics
P.O. Box 5076
Champaign, IL 61825-5076
800-747-4457
e-mail: humank@hkusa.com

Canada: Human Kinetics
475 Devonshire Road Unit 100
Windsor, ON N8Y 2L5
800-465-7301 (in Canada only)
e-mail: orders@hkcanada.com

Europe: Human Kinetics
107 Bradford Road
Stanningley
Leeds LS28 6AT, United Kingdom
+44 (0) 113 255 5665
e-mail: hk@hkeurope.com

Australia: Human Kinetics
57A Price Avenue
Lower Mitcham, South Australia 5062
08 8277 1555
e-mail: liaw@hkaustralia.com

New Zealand: Human Kinetics
Division of Sports Distributors NZ Ltd.
P.O. Box 300 226 Albany
North Shore City
Auckland
0064 9 448 1207
e-mail: blairc@hknewz.com

Welcome to Sports Fundamentals

The Sports Fundamentals Series uses a learn-by-doing approach to teach those who want to play, not just read. Clear, concise instructions and illustrations make it easy to become more proficient in the game or activity, allowing readers to participate quickly and have more fun.

Between the covers, this book contains rock-solid information, precise instructions, and clear photos and illustrations that immerse readers in the heart of the sport. Each fundamental chapter is divided into four major sections:

- You Can Do It!: Jump right into the game or activity with a clear explanation of how to perform an essential skill or tactic.
- More to Choose and Use: Find out more about the skill or learn exciting alternatives.
- Take It to the Lane: Apply the new skill in a game situation.
- Give It a Go: Use drills and game-like activities to develop skills by doing and gauge learning and performance with self-tests.

No more sitting on the sidelines! The Sports Fundamentals Series gets you right into the game. Apply the techniques and tactics as you learn, and have fun—win or lose!

Contents

Introduction

Bowling is one of the greatest recreational sports. Whether you choose to open bowl—that is, bowl with some friends from time to time—or decide to join a bowling league, the social value of bowling is one of its greatest gifts.

One of the many attributes of the game is that people of all skill levels can play, with a maximum of two shots per frame, regardless of where the ball goes on the lane. And the greatest quality is that people of all generations can play. Children, parents, spouses, and grandparents can bowl together. How many other sports have this feature?

Once you realize how great bowling is, you most likely will decide to bowl in a league. Leagues come in many forms, both unsanctioned and sanctioned. The American Bowling Congress (ABC), the Women's International Bowling Congress (WIBC), and the Young American Bowling Alliance (YABA) sanction leagues for men, women, and youth at your local bowling center. In recent years, High School Bowling USA (HSBUSA) and Collegiate Bowling USA (CBUSA) have provided great opportunities for adolescent and young adult bowlers to participate in organized play.

Belonging to a sanctioned league requires that you pay a nominal yearly fee and entitles you to many benefits. For one, the lane conditions are standardized for scoring. Also, you qualify to receive awards for scores that you bowl. Bowling in a sanctioned league qualifies you to bowl in ABC, WIBC, or YABA tournaments throughout the year.

In general, prime league season, though it is referred to as "fall" league season, runs from late summer to mid spring. Bowling proprietors have become creative in offering various league formats and lengths to accommodate the growing demands on people's time. These choices make it easier for many to commit time to bowling on a regular basis.

Bowling is both recreational and competitive at many different levels. Many leagues maintain a portion of the weekly fees collected from bowlers to distribute prize funds at the end of the year, based on team and individual standings. Rather than bowl for money, youth bowlers compete for scholarship funds to help pay for college.

For bowlers who have a more competitive spirit, various amateur clubs and associations host a schedule of tournaments throughout the year: team and individual tournaments, handicapped tournaments, and some scratch tournaments. Competitions often are held on weekends. Bowling centers, sanctioning organizations, or various amateur clubs can host these competitions. The host determines the entry fee, prize fund, and tournament format. In paying your entry fee, you agree to the terms of competition.

The ABC and WIBC have created USA Bowling for those who enjoy the game more, for those who desire to improve their level of play, and for aspiring competitive bowlers. USA Bowling is the governing organization that certifies coaches to make coaching accessible to all bowlers who strive to improve their skills. USA Bowling governs Team USA, the national amateur team. Team USA is formed each year through regional and state qualifying events that culminate in the national finals, the USA Bowling National Amateur Championship (NAC).

Although the national team may not be the goal of many bowlers, many bowlers do enjoy the game when they score more. The USA Bowling Coaching program is recognized by the United States Olympic Committee and certifies Bronze, Silver, and Gold coaches who are qualified to coach bowlers of various skill levels. This program truly provides bowlers a way to improve skills. Seek out a USA Bowling Coaching certified coach in your area to help you work on your skills. It can be very rewarding, inspiring, and satisfying to your game. With three coaching levels, there is always a way to take your game to the next level. Even professionals get coaching to help them improve their skills.

The Professional Bowlers Association (PBA) and the Professional Women's Bowling Association (PWBA) are the professional organizations for elite male and female bowlers. The professionals are among the very best in the world. The PBA and PWBA provide tournament schedules each year and have requirements for joining and maintaining both regional and national memberships. The finals of the national tours are televised.

Bowling is a great game, with so much to offer. It is no wonder that bowling is the highest participation sport in the United States.

Bowling Lane

A bowling lane (figure 1) is 60 feet long from the foul line to the pins. The lane is made up of 39 boards. Generally, right-handed bowlers count the boards from right to left; left-handed bowlers count the boards from left to right. The seven arrows on the lane are spaced five boards apart. They are used as targets. The first arrow on the right

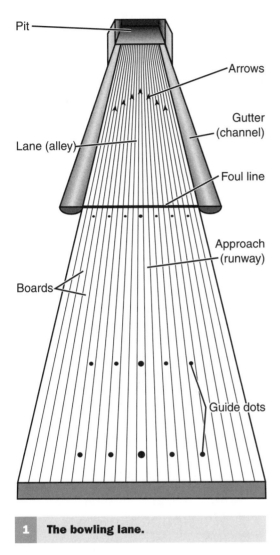

Pit

Arrows

Gutter
(channel)

Lane (alley)

Foul line

Approach
(runway)

Boards

Guide dots

1 **The bowling lane.**

is the fifth board, the second arrow is the tenth board, and so on. Lefties count arrows from the left side in a similar fashion. The dots a couple feet into the lane are also used for targeting, although most bowlers prefer to use the arrows. Some bowlers draw an imaginary line from the dots on the lane to the arrows to form a line to roll on.

Using the arrows is the preferred method of targeting because of their distance from the foul line. The pins are 60 feet away from the foul line, but the targets are only 15 feet away. In a game of accuracy, a closer target is easier to hit consistently than a target that is farther away.

The seven dots at the foul line line up exactly with the arrows. Their board numbers are the same as the arrows.

The approach is 15 feet long. At the back of the approach are two sets of dots. They are used for reference to guide you to start in the same place each time. This does not mean that it is necessary to start directly on either set of dots in the stance; they only serve as reference points. You must start at the appropriate distance from the foul line to match your personal cadence and stride for optimal leverage at delivery.

There may be five or seven dots in each set of dots on the approach. The number of dots is not standard in bowling. When there are five dots on the back of the approach, they are lined up with the inner five arrows on the lane. The first dot on an approach with only five dots, would be the tenth board on the lane and line up with the second arrow. If the approach has seven dots, the dots align with all seven arrows on the lane. Therefore, the first dot would be the fifth board.

Lane conditioner is applied to the lane in the form of oil. The lane is cleaned, then oil is applied by a machine that goes down the lane and back. The oil can be applied in any pattern, much as a golf course has its fairways and sand traps. Tougher conditions usually are created during tournaments. For recreational leagues and open bowling, the oil pattern is basic: a heavy amount of oil in the center of the lane and less on the outside toward the gutters. This facilitates scoring because if a bowler accidentally pulls the shot to the inside of the target, the heavy oil toward the middle of the lane will make the ball slide, or "hold" the ball to the pocket. If a right-handed bowler delivers the ball to the right of the target, it will roll more because of the increased friction out to the right and find its way back to the pocket. With a lot of oil toward the center of the lane and less oil toward the gutters, it is easier to hit the pocket consistently when your shot is lined up on the oil line.

Pins

The pins are arranged according to number, starting with the head pin. The head pin (1) is in the front center of the rack. From the 1 pin, the pins are numbered in rows from left to right, moving toward the back of the rack (figure 2).

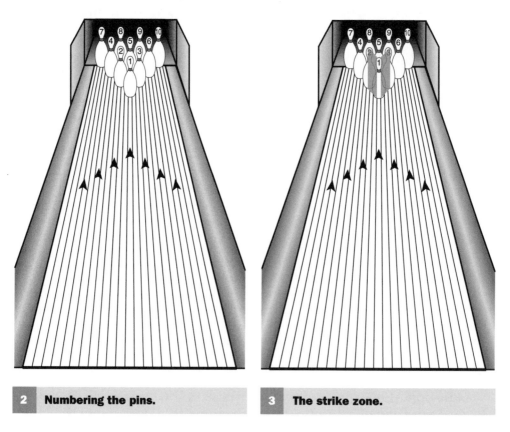

2　**Numbering the pins.**　　　　**3**　**The strike zone.**

The pocket, or strike zone, in bowling is either between the 1 and 3 pins or between the 1 and 2 pins (figure 3). The 1-3 is the pocket to the right side of the head pin; the 1-2 is the pocket to the left side of the head pin. The 1-3 is typically referred to as the right-hand pocket, and the 1-2 is referred to as the left-hand pocket, because right-handers count boards from the right and left-handers count from the left. (The exception is bowlers who throw a reverse hook. These bowlers use the pocket on the opposite side because of the reverse rotation of the reverse hook.) The pocket is on board 17.5, whether you are counting from the right or the left.

To determine the type of release you use, refer to chapter 2. Once you identify the release, you can determine which side to count the arrows from by identifying the proper pocket to use.

Bowling Ball

The cover of the bowling ball is important to performance. The first bowling balls were made of rubber, and later plastic, until technology introduced urethane to the bowling world in the 1980s. Now urethane covers have been upgraded with an additive to the cover stock called reactive resin. Some reactive resin bowling balls even have particles added to their cover stock that add even more traction between the ball and the lane to provide more hook for a bowler who has a hook release. Reactive resin or particle cover stock bowling balls are the preferred bowling balls. They grip the lane better and hit harder than plastic balls.

With technology, bowling balls, like golf clubs, have become stronger. Golf clubs hit farther; bowling balls hook more. Because of this, bowling centers have to put much more oil on the lane to keep up with the traction of the average bowling ball. More oil makes the ball slide, so older balls and plastic balls hook very little under today's conditions.

Many kids start out with a plastic ball (many balls now come with cartoon characters on them). This is better than using a house ball that does not fit, and it's often economical because of the many ball weight changes that a child goes through. Advanced bowlers should purchase a ball that can hook. Many seniors still bowl with their old plastic balls, not realizing the difference the cover can make on performance. The house balls provided by the bowling center are plastic balls. They do not hook much because they do not create much friction with the lane. But because they don't hook much, plastic balls can be useful for shooting spares, particularly corner-pin spares.

Since bowling ball manufacturers know that not every bowler wants to make a substantial financial commitment to bowling, they have created different price ranges for quality balls, including entry-level reactive bowling balls, to encourage the purchase of a reactive resin ball rather than plastic. An entry-level reactive resin or a reactive resin particle ball is a good investment. The cost should be around $100, depending on ball choice and the pricing at the local pro shop. The performance of a reactive resin ball is superior to that of plastic or urethane because of the characteristics of the ball. The outside of a reactive resin ball enhances both the friction created with the lane and the ball's hitting power at the pins.

The cost of a bowling ball includes a fee for drilling finger holes. Proper fit is essential to performance. A poor ball fit will hinder performance; a good ball fit will enhance performance. A local International Bowling Pro Shop and Instructors Association (IBPSIA) certified pro shop can provide a customized ball fit.

Bowling Shoes

Bowling shoes are available for a rental fee at the bowling center. These are basic shoes that are sanitized between rentals. Rentals are a couple dollars, so if you bowl on a regular basis, purchasing a pair of shoes may make economical sense, and you'll have your own pair of shoes that no one else wears.

In the bowling shoes market, you get what you pay for. Bowling shoes come in two basic forms: recreational and performance shoes. Performance shoes are available at various prices based on features. With house and recreational shoes, the soles of both the right and left foot are identical. Performance shoes come in right- or left-hand variations. The slide foot has a buckskin-type sole and the push-off foot has a rubber sole for traction on the approach. Premium performance shoes typically provide a stronger base of support to the feet than less expensive bowling shoes provide.

Performance shoes are available for less than twice the price of recreational shoes. You can purchase a quality-brand shoe with superior performance and wear for around $100. Spend more and you can get performance shoes that come with changeable soles that have Velcro and a variety of attachable bottoms. These are great if you bowl in different centers; these shoes will help you achieve the same slide on the last step regardless of the type and texture of the approach. Decide on your budget for bowling. When it comes to bowling shoes, when you spend more, you do get more. As with any sport, good shoes can be a great investment.

Other Supplies

Most bowlers need some form of wrist support. Wrist guards that provide adequate support have metal bars inside that span from the arm over the wrist joint to the knuckles of the hand to stablize the wrist during the shot.

A good, basic wrist guard costs approximately $15 to $25, depending on the material. When you spend more, some wrist guards provide more support because they are longer, extending to the fingers. Some wrist guards are so elaborate—particularly the bulky plastic or metal wrist guards—that they change the span of your hand; therefore, you should wear them when you're fitted for a ball.

The best advice is to consult the pro shop professional or your coach to determine which wrist guard will offer the best support while improving your particular release. All wrist guards have different levels of support and different functions. The wrist is such a small joint, and for many bowlers basic support is better than no support at all.

Two other supplies to have in your bowling bag include bowling tape and bowling ball cleaner, available in the pro shop. You put bowling tape in the thumbhole to make it smaller if your thumb is smaller than normal. This gives you a good grip and prevents you from squeezing the ball. A relaxed hand is the key to a relaxed swing! Your pro shop professional or coach can help you learn how to use tape. A pocketknife, small screwdriver, or a pair of scissors will aid in putting the tape into the hole.

If you own a reactive resin ball, bowling ball cleaner will be one of the best investments you can make. Reactive resin balls create friction on the lane to cut through the oil and, as a result, also absorb the oil. Cleaning out the pores after every outing will maintain the performance and improve the lifespan of the ball. These cleaners are user friendly; with a napkin or towel, apply the cleaner to the ball and wipe it thoroughly. Look at the towel. Where there is dirt, there is oil—oil that was on the ball to hinder friction! Again, have a professional advise you on the proper cleaner for your ball.

Step Onto the Lane

Bowling Fundamentals will shape your approach to the game. Develop your physical game on the approach. Learn to use your whole body to bowl rather than just your hand and arm. Learn how to loosen up and let your body bowl. Learn to walk naturally and swing loosely to bowl better. Once you coordinate the ball with your feet, just let yourself flow to better scores. In this process of learning to bowl better, keep this in mind: Your swing is the key. The better your swing, the better your game!

Also, learn how to approach the lane with techniques to establish or improve your average. Learn how to line up and target, adjust to hit the pocket, and pick up spares more consistently. Hitting the pocket, leaving fewer pins to pick up, and picking up the spares that remain are the keys to increasing your average.

Get ready to enjoy bowling and the friendships and bonds that you will create as a result of participating in this great sport. Play your hardest and get hooked. You will find that the more you play, the more you want to play and learn about the game. That is the sign of a truly enjoyable sport.

Welcome to *Bowling Fundamentals.*

Gripping the Bowling Ball

Successful bowling requires balance between power and consistency. To develop consistency, you need a relaxed, natural arm swing. A natural swing is easiest to repeat. To keep tension out of the swing, you also must have the proper grip on the ball.

Both a good ball fit and the application of proper grip pressure have a major impact on the swing. In other words, to develop a consistent swing you need a ball that fits properly and you need to apply minimal grip pressure throughout the entire play, including the stance, approach, and delivery (release point). This will lead to better consistency and accuracy.

It is also important to use a ball that is the correct weight. If the ball is too light, it can be overpowered by the arm, inhibiting the pendulum effect; if the ball is too heavy, it is difficult to develop a full and loose arm swing. With ball fit and ball weight in mind, you need to decide whether to purchase a ball or not. Owning your own ball is advised. When you purchase your own ball you have the advantage of choosing one that is a proper weight and fit for you. Also, the quality of the ball, particularly the ball's cover, can help you achieve optimal performance.

Get a Grip

The two types of grips are the conventional grip and the fingertip grip. Most bowlers begin with the conventional grip, eventually graduating to a fingertip grip.

Each finger (not including the thumbs) has two joints. For ease of reference, think of the joint nearest the fingertip as the first joint and the joint in the middle of the finger as the second joint. In a conventional grip, the fingers go into the holes up to the second joint in the middle of the finger. On a ball that is drilled for a conventional grip, the finger holes are closer to the thumb and are larger to accommodate the size of the fingers up to the second joint. Once the fingers are in, the thumb should go into the hole all the way to the base of the thumb (figure 1.1). Most bowlers start out with a conventional grip because it makes them feel more secure when swinging the ball. More finger in the ball initially feels more secure.

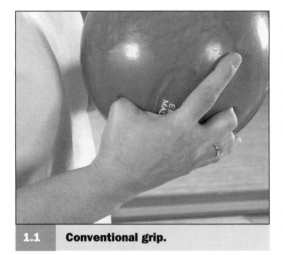

1.1   Conventional grip.

In the fingertip grip (figure 1.2), the fingers go into the holes up to the first finger joint. On a ball that is drilled for a fingertip grip, the finger holes are drilled farther from the thumb, compared to a conventional grip, and the holes are smaller to accommodate the smaller size of just the fingertips from the first joint to the tip. Once the fingers are in, the thumb should go into the hole all the way to the base of the thumb.

In the fingertip grip, the ball has more time over the fingers, which can create more roll on the ball. A fingertip grip will eventually be the preferred grip because it allows you to create more revolutions in the way the ball rolls. It is a myth that a fingertip grip

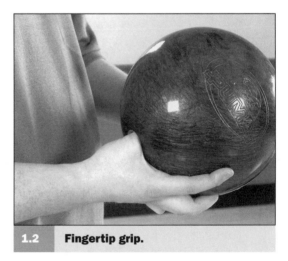

1.2   Fingertip grip.

makes it more difficult to hold on to the ball. If the ball fits properly, you can easily hold on to the ball with a fingertip grip.

With both grips, the thumb exits before the fingers during release (chapter 7). Therefore, the length of time from thumb release to finger release varies between the two grips because of the amount of hand spanning over the ball.

To maintain a loose, natural arm swing, use a minimal amount of grip pressure to hold on to the ball. With a proper fit, both fingers should be able to go into the ball all the way to the proper joint, depending on grip type, and the thumb should go into the thumb hole all the way (figure 1.3). If the thumb does not go all the way in, the grip will feel insecure and you will tend to squeeze the ball. If the thumb cannot go all the way in, either the thumb hole is too tight or the distance from the finger holes to the thumb hole, called the span, is too far.

1.3   **Thumb goes in all the way.**

Most bowlers start out with a conventional grip because it initially feels like a more secure grip. Once you develop an established level of consistency—typically when you average around 140—a fingertip grip becomes the preferred grip. At this level, you are hitting the pocket and picking up spares more consistently and need to begin developing more pin action on the ball's impact at the pocket. A fingertip grip will help you strike more as well as create better pin count on the first shot to leave easier spares (with fewer pins) to pick up on the second shot.

Although the fingers and thumb release closer together in a conventional grip, a fingertip grip creates more revolutions on the ball. With less of your fingers in the ball, the thumb clears much sooner than the fingers to impart more revolutions to the ball. In a conventional grip, the fingers exit more slowly, delaying the transfer of weight to the fingers and decreasing revolutions. Releasing from a fingertip grip creates a quicker transfer of ball weight from the thumb to the fingers to impart more roll off the fingers at release. Bowlers with higher averages and professional bowlers (with few exceptions) use a fingertip grip for its superior effect on the roll of the ball. That is what creates better pin action when the ball strikes the pocket.

Properly putting the hand in the ball—a properly fitted ball—is important to being able to maintain proper grip pressure throughout the swing. To put the hand in properly, first put the fingers in all the way to the proper joint, then fully insert the thumb (figure 1.4).

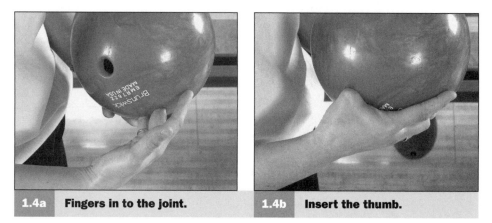

| 1.4a | Fingers in to the joint. | 1.4b | Insert the thumb. |

Don't Squeeze Squeezing the ball does not lead to good performance. Holding the ball and squeezing the ball require two differing pressures. Gently hold the ball, keeping the thumb straight in the hole with the palm side of the thumb flush against the hole. Squeezing, or

| 1.5 | Minimal pressure, proper grip. |

clenching, the ball occurs when the hand is tense. The joint of the thumb then flexes in the hole and puts pressure against the back of the hole with the knuckle and against the front of the hole with the tip of the thumb. In fact, squeezing the ball only creates tension throughout the swing and delays the thumb's exit from the ball at release. The thumb should exit first for a good release.

For example, consider a golfer who holds on to the club harder than usual. Will the golfer hit the ball farther? Definitely not. In golf as well as bowling, the power of the shot is in the mechanics, not the grip pressure.

Once the hand is properly fitted into the ball, the fingers and thumb should be able to hold on to the ball with minimal pressure, much like holding onto a baby bird. In the stance, holding the ball firmly without squeezing is important (figure 1.5). This will set the tone for the entire swing. Keep the grip pressure constant throughout the swing. Centrifugal force will take over during the swing to keep the ball firmly on the hand so that you won't have to squeeze it.

The same amount of grip pressure should be maintained, not increased, at the release point. This will keep the swing consistent throughout the entire approach, including the delivery. Keeping the thumb relaxed will allow it to clear the ball easily, further allowing the weight to transfer over the fingers to impart spin at release.

Because the hand is vital to the swing, excessive grip pressure only leads to inconsistency in the swing and the release. Being relaxed is the only true way to be able to repeat shots. Power comes from body position in the form of leverage at delivery and the wrist and hand motion at release.

Choose the Right Ball   One difference between golf and bowling is that in golf one is taught how to hold a club. In bowling, a grip is provided in the drilling of the holes into the ball. If the grip is poor, the bowler has to squeeze the ball with excessive pressure. A quality fit enables a bowler to relax the hand during the swing.

1.6   **Proper tension.**

When the fingers and the thumb are all the way in the ball, the palm should lie across the ball with neither too much nor too little tension in the web of the thumb (figure 1.6). The holes should be the size of the fingers and thumb. You should be able to put the hand into the ball easily. The holes should not be so tight as to inhibit putting them in all the way, nor should they be so loose you have to squeeze the ball to hold on to it. With a proper fit, maintaining gentle grip pressure, without excessive squeezing, will be much easier.

Choose the heaviest ball you can throw without compromising your ability to have a full, relaxed arm swing, good speed, and a firm wrist at the release. A general rule is to throw 1 pound of ball per 10 pounds body weight, then add 1 pound. For example, a typical 120-pound bowler would consider throwing a 12- or 13-pound ball. There are exceptions, because physical strength and skill also need to be taken into consideration.

Once identifying the ball weight this formula suggests, you can further choose a ball of the proper weight by extending your arms in front of you and having another person place the ball into your hands (figure 1.7). The weight should not pull you off balance or make you lose your posture. Then try a heavier ball. Use the heaviest weight that does not compromise your body position.

1.7 **Find the right weight.**

Although a heavier ball can have more power on impact at the pins, more weight is not always better. Using a weight that causes you to labor over a good pushaway or letting the ball swing will compromise the power, speed, and consistency of the swing itself. Maintaining good ball speed is important. Your ability to handle the ball's weight is critical at the beginning of the swing, or the pushaway (see chapter 2). Allowing the weight to swing over the full arc of the swing also requires strength. A full back swing is integral to power and ball speed.

Finally, it takes strength to maintain a firm wrist position at the release. Frequently, bowlers who begin to throw the ball with more speed decide immediately to increase ball weight without realizing the effects that ball weight has on the wrist position and release.

Professional bowlers have both good speed and a strong wrist action to create revolutions. And many professionals do not even throw 16-pound balls because of the effect ball weight has on the wrist position and release, proving that more is not always better!

Purchase Your Own Bowling Ball   At your local bowling center, the "house" balls come in various weights and sizes and are generically produced to accommodate the masses of recreational bowlers. If you bowl on a regular basis, owning a ball is an advisable option because the ball is personalized to suit your hand. You're more likely to have a ball with the appropriate fit and weight if you purchase one. The right weight and fit facilitate proper grip pressure, leading to a better swing and better overall performance.

When you go to a reputable pro shop for a personalized fit, not only will the span and hole size be tailored to your hand, but so will the angles of the holes as they are drilled into the ball. The angle of each hole, called pitch, is contoured to compliment both the length and flexibility of the hand. Correct pitches not only provide better comfort but also aid in your attempt to apply only sufficient, not excessive, grip pressure.

If you purchase your own ball, you can make sure the cover of the ball is of good quality. For a ball to be able to hook, it must create friction with the lane. The cover of the ball determines the amount of friction the ball will create on the lane. The lane is covered with oil, which makes the ball slide. The more oil there is on the lane, the stronger the cover of the ball needs to be to create friction with the lane. When throwing a hook—imparting spin on the ball at the release—you want to throw a ball that is able to create enough friction to hook. Different bowling balls have different hook potentials.

To understand hook potential, think of bowling balls as tires on a vehicle. Some tires have more tread than others to create friction with the road. Plastic balls (figure 1.8a) are like bald tires; that is, they have very little tread on them, so they create little friction with the lane. Performance balls (figure 1.8b) have urethane covers that contain reactive resin, an additive that makes the ball grab the lane better and hit the pins harder. Reactive resin balls are like tires with good tread on them; these balls create more friction on the lane the way good tires create better traction on the road. Thus, they are considered more aggressive than plastic bowling balls. Reactive resin balls come with various "treads" on them, depending on the amount of friction a bowler wants to create on the lane.

1.8a Plastic ball.

1.8b Performance ball.

Having a ball with the right amount of hook for the way you throw the ball is important. There is a trade-off point when it comes to control, so more friction is not always better. Think about how comfortable you feel when you see the ball hook and how much hook you like to see. Consulting a reputable pro shop to purchase the right ball with a good fit is a great option if you have the budget for it.

If you bowl regularly, a plastic ball that fits you is better than just any house ball. An entry-level performance ball is an even better option for creating enough friction on the lane to see the ball roll more while creating better pin action on impact. Reactive resin balls hit the pins better than plastic balls do. This helps you relax the swing because you don't feel that you have to try to make the ball hook. Eventually, a fingertip grip will be the preferred grip so that you can create more roll on the ball for better pin action.

Let It Swing

The most common problem among bowlers is a muscled arm swing caused by excessive grip pressure. Bowlers who try too hard generally apply more grip pressure to either aim the ball or make it hook. In either case, the excessive grip pressure only leads to inconsistency in the arm swing. The muscles of both the hand and arm end up tight, leading to a controlled, unnatural arm swing. A controlled swing will become erratic as the result of varying tensions in the muscles of the arm at various points throughout the swing. This is why it is important to grip the ball properly, putting the thumb in all the way. Some bowlers fear that they will not be able to get their thumb out of the ball at release, so they put the thumb only partially into the ball. This actually has the reverse effect, creating a less secure grip and causing bowlers to squeeze the ball more to hold onto it. This creates inconsistency in the swing as well as in the release.

Rather than trying to aim the ball, trust your natural swing to make you more accurate. In league play, every bowler strives to hit the target. Too many bowlers try too hard to hit the target by forcing the swing and release rather than relying on natural hand–eye coordination, which will actually produce better accuracy than controlling it ever could. This is not to say that a bowler cannot force hitting the target from time to time by steering the ball. However, over time, the key to developing a higher average is to develop consistency in making shots, and a natural swing will be the most repeatable tactic.

To hit a mark consistently requires a natural arm swing. If your swing is erratic while you're trying to score, your tendency will be to try harder rather than try better. Trying to relax and let the ball swing requires more trust than most bowlers are willing to concede. Most bowlers want to control the ball. That effort creates the tension that makes their swings more erratic.

Relaxing enough to allow the ball to swing naturally will provide any bowler the desired accuracy. But, effortwise, the feeling required to let the ball just swing often leaves a bowler feeling lazy or aloof. The truth is that a loose swing will be more consistent than a tight swing, and a loose swing is closely related to grip pressure. It is a matter of trust, not force. In later chapters, the technique for developing power while maintaining a loose swing for consistency will be addressed.

Often, if bowlers are not gripping the ball too hard to force it toward the target, they grip it harder in an effort to try to hook it more. That is detrimental to a healthy and accurate arm swing. If the ball is not hooking enough, perhaps it is the release, which is in the motion of the wrist and hand. This will be covered in chapter 7. If the release isn't the problem, then perhaps there is more oil on the lane than the ball can handle. Using a ball that creates enough friction on the lane is essential for a ball to be able to hook. The point is that hand and wrist rotation and ball surface create hook, not grip pressure. Excessive grip pressure only creates an inconsistent arm swing.

Conversely, the lanes could be very dry and the ball might be creating too much friction with the lane, making it hook too much. In this situation, many bowlers will try to force the ball down the lane, increasing grip pressure in the process. Using a ball with a cover that creates less friction with the lane is a better option for cutting down hook. This will allow the ball to get down the lane naturally so that you can keep the swing relaxed enough to hit the target consistently.

Give it a go

BALL IN HAND

If the ball fits properly, the fingers will be able to go into the ball to the appropriate joint and the thumb will be able to insert completely into the thumb hole (figure 1.9). The thumb should be able to go to the base without the fingers pulling out of the holes. If you can insert the fingers and thumb easily and fully into the ball, then the grip is at least decent.

1.9   Proper fit.

1.10 **Natural swing, no squeezing.**

GOOD GRIP PRESSURE

If the ball is a proper fit, grip pressure should be minimal. Use the following drill to test the grip and see whether the ball will stay on your hand without squeezing it.

Take a practice swing. Standing still, hold the ball by your side with both hands supporting the weight of the ball. Push the ball forward with both hands and let it swing naturally by your side without excessively squeezing the ball (figure 1.10). Can you do this without dropping the ball? If the natural force of the swing keeps the ball on your hand, you will be able to achieve a relaxed, consistent arm swing.

BOWLING TAPE

If you feel you have to grip the ball when you swing it, try using bowling tape in the holes. Bowling tape is available in pro shops and sometimes in vending machines at the bowling center. Inserting bowling tape into the thumb hole will make the hole more snug to accommodate the natural fluctuations in thumb size (figure 1.11). It can be inserted or removed as necessary. Fluctuations in thumb size occur because of fluid intake, temperature, and humidity. Bowling tape will make the ball fit the hand better during every shot.

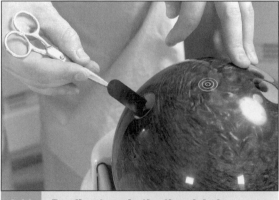

1.11 **Bowling tape in the thumb hole.**

Next Frame

Proper ball weight and grip are essential to a loose and full arm swing. Putting the fingers into the ball to the proper joint, whether in a conventional or a fingertip grip, while being able to easily insert the thumb completely are essential to a good grip. Hole sizes must be snug enough to avoid excessive squeezing. If you can push the ball away and let it swing freely for a loose swing, you have an adequate ball fit.

Many bowlers want to grip the ball too hard, trying too hard to aim the ball or hook it. Neither aim nor hook is achieved by holding the ball harder. Trying harder only creates tension, and that tension will make the swing inconsistent. Aiming the ball is the product of a tight arm swing. Forcing the ball to a target is the quickest way to develop inconsistency and inaccuracy! To hook a ball, get the body into a position of strong leverage at the foul line, imparting rotation to the ball with the proper wrist motion. The following chapters address the proper techniques to achieve this. Simply put, gripping the ball harder does not lead to better scores.

Once you are comfortable and ready, try a fingertip grip. This also would be a good time to get a reactive resin ball for better performance. A good ball fit that allows you to put your hand into the ball properly will facilitate proper grip pressure. Use bowling tape to keep the thumb hole snug so that you do not have to grip the ball. This will help you maintain a loose arm swing. Use a ball that will create the proper friction on the lane so that you do not have to force the ball down the lane or try to force it to hook. These techniques will help you achieve better consistency and accuracy.

Finding Your Stance

The starting position, or stance, sets the tone for the motion that follows. Knowing how and where to stand is important for a good delivery. Starting from a position of leverage in a relaxed body position will lead you to a successful approach.

Determining where to stand involves two factors: how far from the foul line to start and which board of the approach to stand on. To create a smooth motion with good rhythm to the foul line, walk naturally during the approach. Many bowlers end up short of the foul line, they overstride, or they end up rushing to the line because they start too far back on the approach. The distance to stand from the foul line on your approach depends on the length of your natural strides.

Your method of release determines which board to start on. The release will cause the ball to roll in one of three directions: clockwise, straight forward, or counterclockwise. The type of roll determines which pocket to use and whether to target on the right or left side of the lane. From there, you can determine where to stand on the approach. See chapter 8 for more information on hitting the pocket. To maximize pin action and minimize ball deflection on impact, use the correct pocket for the way your ball rolls.

Establishing Stance Position

2.1   **Side view of the stance.**

In the stance, stand with the feet together and the knees slightly bent to feel ready to move (figure 2.1). Flexed joints move more easily than stiff joints. The body should be relaxed and ready to move. The spine should have a slight tilt to it, about 15 degrees, to maintain a naturally strong leverage position. The body is in a good leverage position when the upper body is over your center of gravity and your weight is distributed over a sound base of support: your feet. The body should feel balanced, ready to move both the starting foot and the ball. To step easily with the starting foot, the majority of the body weight should be on the nonstarting foot.

Start with the right foot slightly behind the left to preset the hips and shoulders as they will be at the delivery (figure 2.2). (Left-handed bowlers will put the left foot slightly behind the right to preset the hips and shoulders.) At delivery for a right-handed bowler, the left foot ends up ahead of the right, setting the hips in an open position. (Left-handers end up on the right foot, setting the hips in an open position.)

Support the weight of the ball with both hands to allow the swing arm to be relaxed during the pushaway. The elbow of the swing arm should be by the side, next to the ribs, and the ball should be held in line with the shoulder (figure 2.3). Keeping the elbow by the side and holding the ball directly forward in line with the shoulder joint will facilitate a straight arm swing.

Many bowlers try to hold the ball close to the middle of the body because this makes it feel lighter. This position prevents

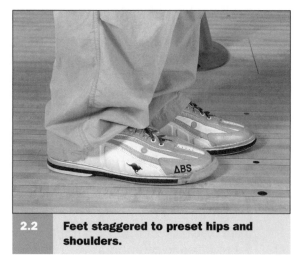

2.2   **Feet staggered to preset hips and shoulders.**

a straight arm swing in line with the shoulder. Holding the ball in line with the shoulder confirms the need to use the opposite hand to support the weight of the ball. Using only the swing arm to support the ball's weight will make the arm swing and shoulder muscles work too hard, and the muscles will become tense. This creates tension in the swing that would otherwise be more consistent if the muscles were more relaxed. Bowlers often start out in the approach more tense than they mean to be or even realize that they are. Tension in the stance can lead to inconsistency in the swing.

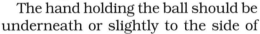

2.3   **Ball in line.**

The hand holding the ball should be underneath or slightly to the side of the ball, whichever is more comfortable. Again, to stay relaxed and keep the arm swing loose throughout the stance and start, support the weight of the ball with both hands. Actually, supporting the weight of the ball primarily with the opposite hand (the left hand for a right-handed bowler) will help keep the muscles of the swing arm and shoulders relaxed. To have a loose arm swing, maintain loose muscles throughout the stance and start.

Generally, positioning the arm with the elbow by the side to hold the ball parallel to the floor is a good position from which to push the ball out in the start. Depending on timing tendencies, you might hold the ball higher or lower in the stance. Holding the ball higher or lower will change the shape of the pushaway in the start.

Once the elbow is set by your side, find a comfortable place to position the ball with the forearm. When holding the ball lower, push it out and slightly up in the start. When holding the ball higher, push it out and slightly down in the start. Changing the height of the ball in the stance may lead to better timing. (This will be addressed more in chapter 5.)

The goal is to set the stance to get the swing shoulder lined up with the appropriate target to hit the pocket. Identifying what type of bowler you are and the best release for you to use is a good starting point. From there, you can fine-tune the angle to the pocket. Chapter 8 provides further details on adjusting angles to hit the pocket.

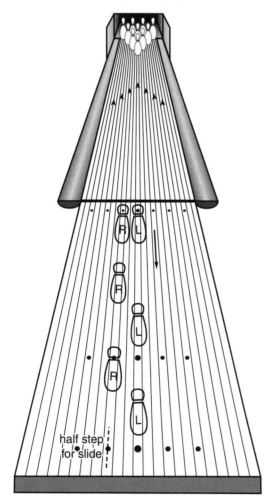

half step
for slide

To determine how far back to stand on the approach, walk up to the foul line and put your heels on the dots with your back to the pins. From the foul line, take four comfortable but brisk steps toward the back of the approach (figure 2.4). After the fourth step, add approximately another half step to allow for the slide. This will determine your approximate starting point for the approach. Again, walk naturally but briskly, because taking normal-sized steps with momentum is the key to a comfortable approach and your ability to repeat shots.

To figure out which board to stand on, you need to identify which type of release you have, which influences the pocket you should use. Your positioning on the lane depends on your swing arm and type of release. The type of release is determined by the direction of rotation imparted to the ball, which in turn determines the best side from which the ball should enter the pins for maximum drive. The ball should spin toward the middle of the rack of pins for minimal deflection on impact, so you can determine your position on the board by the rotation of the ball.

A ball that does not curve or significantly spin in either direction and whose path is virtually straight down the lane with a forward roll is called a straight ball. It does not hook in one direction or another. A right-handed bowler with a straight ball will use the 1-3 pocket.

For the right-handed bowler, a ball that curves from right to left is a hook. Another way to define hook

2.4   **Determining how far back to stand.**

is a ball that spins in a counterclockwise direction. A right-handed bowler with a hook will use the 1-3 pocket to maximize drive into the pocket into the pins on impact.

The exception to a right-hander using the 1-3 pocket and counting the arrows from the right is the bowler who throws a reverse spin, or back-up ball. A ball that curves from left to right is a reverse hook. The reverse hook of a right-handed bowler spins in a clockwise direction. To minimize ball deflection, bowlers who throw a reverse hook use the 1-2 pocket to maximize the drive of the ball into the pins. With a spin like that of a left-handed hook, this bowler will count the arrows from left to right as a left-handed bowler counts the arrows from left to right.

Basically, right-handed bowlers use the right 1-3 pocket and count the arrows from the right side of the lane to the target on the right side of the lane. Left-handers use the left 1-2 pocket and count the arrows from the left side to the target on the left side. The exception is the bowler who throws a reverse hook, or back-up ball (see tables 2.1 and 2.2). These bowlers will use the opposite pocket, counting the arrows and target from the opposite side of the lane because of the reverse spin on the ball. Also, bowlers should use the foot they end on at the finish to line up the stance on the approach. For right-handed bowlers, this is the left foot; for left-handers, this is the right foot.

TABLE 2.1 RIGHT-HAND RELEASES

	Straight	Hook	Reverse hook*
Direction ball curves	Doesn't curve	Right to left	Left to right
Direction ball rotates	Doesn't rotate	Counterclockwise	Clockwise
Pocket to use	1-3	1-3	1-2
Target	Right side	Right side	Left side

*Count arrows from left side.

TABLE 2.2 LEFT-HAND RELEASES

	Straight	Hook	Reverse hook*
Direction ball curves	Doesn't curve	Left to right	Right to left
Direction ball rotates	Doesn't rotate	Clockwise	Counterclockwise
Pocket to use	1-2	1-2	1-3
Target	Left side	Left side	Right side

*Count arrows from right side.

A right-handed bowler who throws a straight ball, whose goal is to put the ball in the 1-3 pocket, will stand just left of the middle dot on the approach. The middle dot is board 20 and it is larger than the other dots. The left foot is approximately on board 23. The arm swing is lined up with the third arrow, and the third arrow is the target (figure 2.5a).

A left-handed bowler who throws a straight ball, whose goal is to put the ball in the 1-2 pocket, will stand just right of the middle dot on the approach. The right foot is approximately on board 23. The arm swing is lined up with the third arrow, and the third arrow is the target (figure 2.5b).

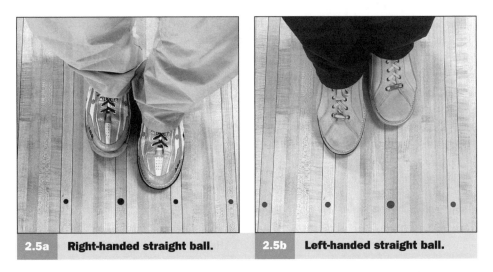

| **2.5a** | **Right-handed straight ball.** | **2.5b** | **Left-handed straight ball.** |

A right-handed bowler who throws a hook ball will use the 1-3 pocket and can begin by standing just right of the center dot (figure 2.6a). The left foot is approximately on board 18, and the target is close to the second arrow. A left-handed bowler who throws a hook ball will use the 1-2 pocket and can begin by standing just left of the center dot (figure 2.6b). The right foot is approximately on board 18, and the target will be close to the second arrow.

A right-hander who throws a reverse hook will line up for the 1-2 pocket. The right-handed bowler lines up using the second or third arrows from the left, with the left foot starting on approximately board 7 from the left (figure 2.7a). It is necessary to stand so far over because the arm swing is on the right side of the body but the pocket and target are on the left side of the lane.

A left-hander who throws a reverse hook will line up for the 1-3 pocket. The left-handed bowler lines up using the second or third arrows from the right, the right foot starting on approximately board 7 from the right (figure 2.7b). It is necessary to stand so far over

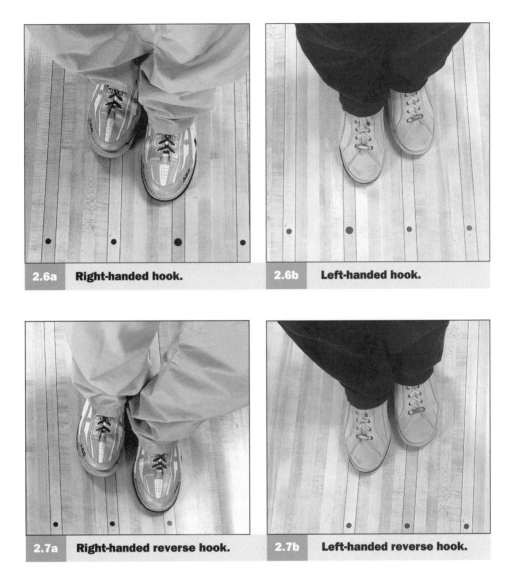

| 2.6a | Right-handed hook. | 2.6b | Left-handed hook. |

| 2.7a | Right-handed reverse hook. | 2.7b | Left-handed reverse hook. |

because the arm swing is on the left side of the body but the pocket and target are on the right side of the lane.

Depending on the quality of the ball and the amount of rotation you impart at release, you may stand slightly right or left of these board numbers in the stance to allow for how much the ball does, or does not, hook. The amount of hook is influenced by the amount of friction that the ball creates with the lane caused by the individual release and the type of ball thrown.

If the release provides more revolutions to create more friction with the lane, then you may need to adjust the relationship of the stance to the target accordingly. If the ball is not coming up to the pocket, then a more direct shot to the pocket is necessary. If the ball rolls past the pocket to the other side of the head pin, then less angle is necessary.

The amount of friction the cover of the ball creates will also influence where you stand in relation to the target. When using a more or less aggressive ball, you may need to adjust the stance according to the amount of friction the ball creates with the lane. Allowing for the ball's reaction on the lane is the key to fine-tuning your position on the approach. Chapter 8 addresses adjusting angles and adjusting to the lane conditions.

Relax on the Approach

Being relaxed is one of the most important keys to creating a consistent approach and delivery. In any game of repetition, staying loose is the key to being able to repeat. Bowlers face the same challenge as a free-throw shooter in basketball. It comes down to repeating the motion over and over. A free-throw shooter will go through a preshot routine to loosen up and get ready to repeat the shot he has done so often. Many bowlers are not aware of how tight their muscles generally are in a normal state.

It is a myth that the shoulders must be perfectly square and even for the upper body to be relaxed. Because you are holding the weight of the ball on one side, it's logical that the shoulder of the swinging arm will be slightly lower than the other shoulder because of the weight of the ball.

If you are having trouble delivering the ball consistently, check to see whether you are holding any tension in the muscles used to hold the ball and the muscles used in the swing. Many bowlers start out with tight muscles in the stance and do not even realize it. Gripping the ball too tightly in the stance creates too much tension in the arm, preventing a loose and consistent arm swing. Many bowlers do not even realize they start out with tight muscles in the forearm, upper arm, and shoulders. Holding the ball too tightly and muscling the arm swing are two major errors keeping bowlers from bowling their best.

If inconsistency and inaccuracy are plaguing you, loosen up and relax your grip. Stand with the muscles relaxed in the stance. Tight hand, arm, or shoulder muscles will prevent you from producing your best swing, which is your most relaxed swing. Stand with your shoulders relaxed, allowing your right shoulder (if right-handed) to be lower than your left because of the weight of the ball. Stay relaxed so that the movement of the ball in the pushaway also produces movement in the upper arm during the swing. The upper arm should move forward in the pushaway so that the arm swing begins momentum that continues to develop throughout the entire approach.

To repeat shots, let the ball swing naturally. With a proper line-up in the stance, natural hand–eye coordination will produce accurate shots if the swing repeats itself every time. And let the thumb just clear at the release point rather than try to help the ball. Most important, trust yourself.

ARE YOU RELAXING IN THE STANCE?

To see whether you're relaxed, put your arm in another person's hand in the same position as it is in the stance. Without the ball, assume your stance position. Relax completely, allowing the other person to support the weight of your arm with his hand beneath your wrist. Have the other person let go. Does your forearm fall to your side? If not, the muscles are keeping it up. For a relaxed stance, the muscles of the arm should be in a relaxed state where the arm would have fallen if the other person withdrew his support of your forearm. In a truly relaxed state, your arm will fall.

TENSE AND RELAX IN STANCE

If you are not sure whether your arm is tense in the stance, you can teach yourself what is relaxed and what is loose by squeezing and relaxing your muscles during the stance. First squeeze your hand and tighten up the muscles of your arm and shoulder. Then release the tension. Notice the difference and take particular note of the feeling when the muscles are relaxed. This is the feeling you want in your stance.

PROGRESSIVE MUSCLE RELAXATION

If you are not sure how to relax, do progressive muscle relaxation drills at home. While lying in bed at night, tense and relax specific body parts, starting with your forehead, working through your face, neck, shoulders, arms, buttocks, legs, and feet. Do not progress to another part of your body until you relax the one you are working on. You may even fall asleep before finishing!

Once you achieve a relaxed state, conjure up an image in your mind that you associate with a relaxed state of being—a sunset, a lake, or whatever makes you think of relaxing. Do this every night for several weeks. Your body will involuntarily begin to associate this image with your relaxed state. It will be able to react to your thought of this image to produce a more relaxed body while bowling.

Next Frame

A good finish begins with a good start. The stance is the position from which the entire approach begins. A relaxed stance is crucial to a smooth motion and a loose arm swing. With the joints slightly flexed, the body is prepared to begin motion. It is easier to start from a relaxed position.

Many bowlers start the stance holding the ball too tightly. Some bowlers begin while tense, unaware of how tight their muscles really are. Others are ready to try hard during the approach. Start in a relaxed state so that you will stay relaxed during the motion to follow.

Finally, in an effort to get ready to swing the ball, too many bowlers underestimate the importance of the opposite hand to the creation of a loose swing. Become aware of how the weight is distributed in the stance and throughout the start. Most bowlers put too much weight toward the swing hand, imposing too much stress on the muscles of the swing arm. In this case, it becomes virtually impossible to create a loose and pure swing.

Footwork and the Approach

To be smooth, you need to walk naturally to the foul line. Taking normal steps allows the body to move freely over the approach, allowing the swing to develop a constant momentum to the foul line. Many bowlers try to take steps that are too big, or they try to take them too methodically. Walk on the approach just as you would walk down the street; this is the key to developing natural momentum that can be repeated from shot to shot.

For consistency in the swing, you need to develop momentum throughout the approach. You can coordinate the swing with the steps by learning to bowl with a four-step approach. Four steps give you adequate time to let the ball swing in sync with the feet throughout the approach without having to rush. Taking fewer than four steps doesn't allow enough time for the swing to flow naturally. Taking too many steps only complicates timing. The four-step approach will help you develop a consistent motion to the foul line.

Four-Step Approach

In a four-step approach, a right-handed bowler starts with the right foot. This causes the bowler to end on the proper foot, the left foot, at the end of the approach. The right-handed bowler simply walks to the foul line in four steps as follows: right, left, right, left.

A left-handed bowler starts with the left foot and ends up on the right foot. The left-handed bowler takes steps left, right, left, right. The strides should be natural and comfortable.

The arm moves in sequence with the feet. In the four-step approach, the ball is in four positions as the bowler steps toward the line. These positions can be referred to as "out, down, back, and through."

The four-step approach begins by moving the ball forward with the first step (figure 3.1a). Pushing the ball away from the body (called the pushaway) is done by moving the ball out toward the pins with the first step. This is the beginning of the approach.

At the end of the pushaway, the ball will begin to swing into the approach. The ball should be down on the second step (figure 3.1b). As the second step makes contact with the floor, the ball should be down by the bowler's side, near the right leg (of a right-handed bowler).

After you move the ball out on step one and down on step two, the ball comes back on the third step (figure 3.1c) as the right leg moves forward for the second time (for a right-handed bowler). The arm will reach the height of the back swing, behind you as you, take the third step with the right foot. This is "back on step three."

3.1a　**Out on one.**

3.1b　**Down on two.**

Finally, the four-step approach is completed as the arm comes through to release and delivers the ball (figure 3.1d). On the fourth step, the left foot for a right-handed bowler, the ball is released and the arm follows through. This is "through on step four." The entire approach, arms in coordination with the feet, is an "out, down, back, and through" motion.

Natural biomechanics will help you repeat shots consistently while generating power. That is the key to efficiency. To be natural, walk on the approach as if you were walking with friends in the shopping mall. This will take care of both the size of the strides and the way the steps are taken. The way you take the steps is integral to your process of naturally repeating shots. The only exception is if you choose to use a slide on the last step of the approach. This will be covered in chapter 7.

Taking natural steps is important for developing natural momentum to the line. Just as in typical walking, you need to take steps from heel to toe in natural strides. In normal walking, you initiate a step by first striking the ground with the heel then transferring body weight through the middle of the foot to the ball of the foot to push off into the next step. The process of walking is a natural way to develop momentum.

For a smooth motion to the foul line, take natural strides. The size of the strides during the approach should be similar to the strides you take while walking. Walking naturally will keep your body comfortable, allowing you to repeat the same motion from shot to shot. To do this, start at the proper distance from the foul line (see chapter 2).

3.1c   **Back on three.**

3.1d   **Through on four.**

Five-Step Approach A popular and successful alternative to a four-step approach is the five-step approach. In the five-step approach, you start with the foot opposite to the one you used in the four-step approach. In a four-step approach, a right-handed bowler starts with the right foot; in a five-step approach, the right-handed bowler starts with the left foot.

The timing of the five-step approach is similar to that of the four-step approach. The only difference is that in a five-step approach, the right-handed bowler steps with the left foot before starting the four-step approach (figure 3.2). The additional step is simply a step to get started. The ball still doesn't move until the right foot steps (the second step in the five-step approach). To keep it clear, some refer to the first step of a five-step approach as the zero step before beginning the four-step approach.

Five-Step Approach

| 3.2a | Left step. | 3.2b | Ball moves with right leg. (second step) |

Some bowlers take a five-step approach simply because it is easier for them to get started. It might just come more naturally. Some bowlers take five steps to develop more momentum to the line. Either can be a good reason to take five steps rather than four. The key is to keep the sequence the same, starting the ball with the right foot for a right-handed bowler or the left foot for a left-handed bowler.

Walk Straight The relationship between the stance position and the target forms an angle for the ball. To maintain the same angle at delivery, walk straight during the approach. Walking diagonally will alter the target line.

To check for a straight walk, first identify which board the foot starts on. Then observe which board you finish on. (A right-handed bowler will end on the left foot; a left-handed bowler will end on the right foot.) If you finish on a board other than the one you started on, you are drifting on the lane.

Poor alignment between the stance position and the target is a common cause of drifting. If the relationship between where you stand and where you target does not form a target line to the pocket, you may have to walk in a crooked line to adjust the angle at the finish. If you walk straight, you should make the target line between your stance and target (while considering how much the ball will hook) form an angle that will produce a pocket hit. Also, if you stand too far to the right or left of the target, you will drift from the board you start on, walking toward the target, to finish on the board from which you can actually hit it. To keep the relationship between the stance and target realistic, stand on a board that is at least 5 boards, but no more than 10 boards, to the left of the target (figure 3.3).

Remember that while the eyes are in the middle of the body, the arm swing is not. The shoulder from which the ball swings is several inches from the head. Centering the target in the middle of the body from the stance position will require the arm to throw the ball across the body or it will require you to drift (a right-handed bowler would drift to the left). Proper line-up helps you walk straight.

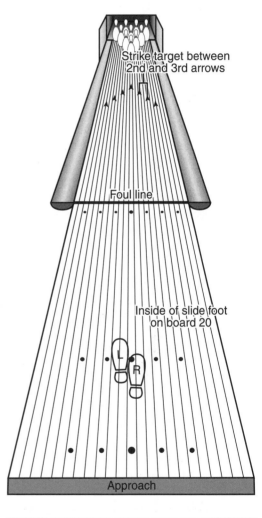

Strike target between 2nd and 3rd arrows

Foul line

Inside of slide foot on board 20

Approach

3.3 Relationship of stance to target. For a right-handed bowler who throws a straight ball, the target is closer to the third arrow; for a hook ball, it's closer to the second arrow.

27

Finishing a board, or even two or three boards, off the start position is not drastic, especially if it is consistent. However, excessive drifting can be corrected with a little overcompensation. If the drift is to the left, trick the mind by exaggerating walking to the right. Although it will feel as if you actually walked to the right, you probably did not end up to the right of your starting position. Compare the starting foot position to the finishing position to determine the actual change. The boards on the approach will serve as a guide to identify the amount of actual drift even if it is contrary to what the body feels. Once you correct the drift, overcompensating thoughts are no longer necessary. Think straight and walk straight!

Avoid Overstriding Many bowlers have a strong tendency to overstride, taking larger steps than necessary. This is an awkward way to walk and affects the normal balance people have when they walk. Often a bowler who overstrides does so because she starts too far back on the approach for the size of her body.

Use the drill in chapter 2 (page 16) to determine where to stand on the approach. Trust your natural stride even if the foul line looks too close. If you are used to starting way back on your approach, you may feel awkward at first when you move up. You may feel cramped for space. It is OK if the first couple of tries feel uncomfortable. You will get used to the new length of the approach.

The key is to learn to take natural steps and eventually the strides will feel more natural. The first couple of tries after moving up, you may even get a foul if your foot goes over the foul line. Once you learn to take more natural strides, you will finish behind the foul line. The delivery will feel more comfortable and the approach will feel more natural. It's a matter of allowing the body weight to stay balanced over the center of the foot while stepping forward. If your body weight shifts too far forward before you take the step, you're likely to overstride as you respond to being off balance and try to catch yourself back into balance.

When the weight transfer through the foot is excessive, extra force is exerted off the ball of the foot when moving into the next step. The push off that step will be too strong, leading to a bigger step. This is a common problem in the beginning of the approach.

Don't Shuffle Avoid taking weak steps or shuffling to the foul line. Shuffling is poor technique from a biomechanics standpoint. When you shuffle, the foot hits the floor flat with the ball of the foot first. This minimizes weight transfer forward through the foot, and the body loses natural momentum to the foul line. Simply put, momentum briefly stops, and this makes the approach less fluid for the swing. Shuffle steps lack power.

To sense the effects of shuffling versus stepping from heel to toe, imagine trying to walk with some friends, keeping up with them while taking shuffle steps. It is virtually impossible to develop any momentum.

Finish Strong   Being uncoordinated at the finish usually originates back to the start. If you are off balance at the finish or have to pull the ball through at the finish, you are out of sync. These are classic symptoms of poor timing.

Finishing with good knee bend and the right leg (if you're a right-hander) behind you to get the hips low, rather than falling off to the side to catch your weight on the right leg, is a sign of good timing. With a good finish, delivering the ball to the target is more consistent and accurate, and the release is stronger. With a good start and a loose swing, the coordination between the footwork and the arm swing should maintain good timing throughout the approach. This will allow the upper body to remain in the same position as in the stance, with only the hips lower at the finish to maintain the leverage to deliver the ball smoothly onto the lane.

Go back to the start to determine where timing becomes poor. If you're a right-handed bowler, move the right arm and right leg together in the start; if you're a left-handed bowler, move the left arm and left leg together in the start. Once the start is synchronized and the ball is pushed out with the first step (four-step approach) or second step (five-step approach), you need only relax the swing and walk naturally. The rest falls into place.

Take it to the lane

Strides and Rhythm

Trying to slow down to control the ball or get it to hook is a common reason bowlers start to shuffle step, unaware of how much biomechanical power is taken away by shuffling. Pick up the feet to generate the rhythm for a fluid swing.

Trouble with rhythm can be a matter of how you are walking. Take a deep breath and work on taking steps naturally. Taking huge steps will stretch the legs out too much and make it more difficult to stay light on your feet. Natural strides that are similar to regular walking are the sign of a relaxed bowler who is letting it happen.

Running to the line with short, choppy steps also will create unnatural walking strides and an increased rhythm to the foul line. It will be difficult to be fluid and create flow to the line. The approach should feel relatively easy to the body. Starting too far from the foul line or trying too hard is often the cause of poor footwork.

Overstriding will make it difficult to feel smooth to the line and often causes inconsistency. Natural strides help you develop a smooth swing. Natural strides and a loose arm swing are the major elements of a smooth approach. And both are necessary to consistently repeat shots.

To keep from overstriding, check how your weight is transferred through the feet while moving out of the stance. Keep balance centered over the middle of the feet in the stance. This will create a calm start and a normal-sized first step. If body weight leans too far forward and gets over the balls of the feet and onto the toes too quickly or abruptly, overstriding will result. If this happens, try keeping the weight back and just walking out of the stance position rather than lunging. This will help your strides become more calm and natural, as they are when you walk down the street.

Give it a go

TEST YOUR RHYTHM AND STRIDE

To see the effect that standing too far back has on rhythm and stride, try standing way back on the approach. Try to get to the line in four natural steps. Unless you are much taller than average, you will end up short of the foul line. You'd have to overstride, maybe even leap, to get to the foul line. This demonstrates that starting too far back on the approach causes an unnatural walk that will create inconsistency.

Now try shuffling all steps. Eventually, you will run out of power to continue. Shuffle steps cause you to decelerate. Now take steps heel to toe. You can accelerate to create momentum, which is the goal of the approach.

CORRECTING DRIFT

To correct drift, place a towel at the foul line with its edge on the board equal to the right or left side of your slide foot in the stance, depending on the direction of your drift. This will encourage your foot to end on the same board that it started on in the stance. If you drift left, put the towel, at the foul line, on the same board that is just left of your slide foot in the stance to force you to slide on the board that you start on. To correct a drift to the right, put the towel on the board that is to the right of your slide foot to force you to slide on the board that you start on. Your body will strive for balance by avoiding slipping on the towel. Repeat many shots with the towel in place at the foul line. This will train your steps to fix your drift.

OUT, DOWN, BACK, AND THROUGH

Without the ball, walk to the foul line, taking four steps and timing your swing to go out, down, back, and through. Practice synchronizing the arm motion to that mantra. You can even try this drill at home. At first, you will be methodical and lack rhythm. Do it many times until you are able to do it correctly. Once you are able to do it correctly, try to do it with natural strides.

As mentioned previously, while learning how to coordinate the feet with the swing when doing this drill, you will be mechanical and methodical. Once you create the proper movement over and over, begin to create a motion that is in time and occurs without pause, which means taking natural walking steps. After you learn to position the ball properly with each step, walking naturally without any pauses between steps will eventually create a flow to the movement. Soon you will be able to do it with rhythm. Then go through the same process with the ball in your hand. It is like learning to ride a bike. First you learn how to do it, then you learn how to stay up without falling, then you eventually learn how to ride with grace in your motion.

To test yourself, stop on any given step and see where the ball is. Is it in the proper position for the step you are on? If not, try again until you can get the swing to move at the right time and into the proper position. If it moves properly, it will not be too quick or too slow to avoid being in the proper position on any given step. At first, put the ball into the proper positions. Eventually, you can do it with natural, uninterrupted speed. Learn to take natural steps to be smooth. Creating the proper synchronization in the approach with a fluid arm swing is the key to a consistent and naturally powerful approach.

Next Frame

The smoothest bowlers walk naturally while swinging the ball loosely. Using the optimal amount of approach rather than more approach is the key. The length of the approach should match the number of steps taken with natural strides. A good step involves striking with the heel first, just as in normal walking.

The four- or five-step approach is preferred to easily synchronize the footwork with the swing. Fewer steps rush the swing; more steps may make it difficult to repeat timing consistently. The only difference between a four- and five-step approach is that in a five-step approach, you take a small step before beginning the four-step approach.

Line up properly to avoid drifting. Standing 5 to 10 boards left of the target (for a right-handed bowler) will line up the shoulder to the target. Walk straight to maintain a good angle between your stance position, the target, and the pocket.

Pushaway and Back Swing

A good, loose arm swing is the cornerstone of good bowling; it helps you achieve high levels of consistency and accuracy. As it has been said, "swing is king." A pure swing leads to consistent shots.

A loose swing will be the most repeatable and will naturally progress from the weight of the ball and the momentum of the approach. The initial movement of the ball from the stance is critical to developing a loose swing. Once the ball is pushed forward at the start of the approach, a loose swing will allow the ball to swing back naturally. This natural momentum will keep the arm on a naturally straight path.

Tension in the swing causes inconsistency and inaccuracy. Trying to muscle the ball rather than letting it swing naturally will make you erratic. Muscles become unpredictable, are capable of tensions in various places throughout the swing, and can cause the ball to swing too little or too much.

Bowlers who try to aim the ball have to use muscle to do it, and the swing becomes tight. The swings of the most accurate players in the world are so loose that they are able to repeat the same motion every time. Your natural swing is your best swing for maintaining a consistent swing height and speed. A tension-free swing will be the most repeatable and the most consistent. A loose swing, in which the ball is pushed at the right time in line with the shoulder, will be a straight, accurate swing.

Keep It Loose

4.1 Nonshooting hand supports the ball.

In the stance, you must be relaxed and loose, setting the tone for the motion to follow. It is difficult to develop a loose swing if the muscles are tense to begin with. The weight of the ball should be distributed over both hands, with most of the ball's weight supported by the hand that is not in the ball (figure 4.1). For a right-handed bowler, this is the left hand.

The position of the opposite hand on the ball depends on the bowler. Some bowlers put the palm on the ball. Others distribute the ball's weight over the fingers. Using the fingers to support the ball rather than placing the entire palm on the ball may be more comfortable. The whole hand or fingers should be on the side or slightly under the ball rather than on top of the ball. The supporting hand won't be able to bear any of the ball's weight if it is on top of the ball.

Put the shooting hand in the ball in the desired position while supporting the weight of the ball with the other hand. Position the shooting hand in the ball first, then find a way to place the nonshooting hand in a supporting position. Slightly behind, under, and to the side of the ball is an effective position for the nonshooting hand.

With the left hand supporting most of the ball's weight, the muscles of the right hand and the swing arm will stay relaxed; they won't have to tense up to support the weight of the ball. Putting the left arm to work not only will allow the muscles of the swing arm to relax during the stance, but it also will be instrumental in helping you develop a consistent and loose arm swing.

The pushaway is the initial movement of the ball from the stance and the beginning of the arm swing. A good pushaway is essential to developing both a loose arm swing and good timing. In a sound pushaway, both hands support the weight of the ball while both arms extend the ball forward to initiate the arm swing (figure 4.2). As described in chapter 3, the pushaway begins with the right leg for a right-handed bowler or the left leg for the left-handed bowler.

During the pushaway, the elbows move forward, away from the sides, to put the ball out in a position from which to swing. This

4.2 **The pushaway begins the arm swing.**

initiates the movement of the upper arm, beginning the swing from the shoulder. You need to move the upper arm and not just the ball in the pushaway.

Supporting the weight of the ball with the nonshooting hand becomes important at the end of the pushaway when the ball is farthest from the body. This is where it will feel the heaviest. Without support from the left hand, the hand and swing arm will become tense as they try to support the heavy weight of the ball. Leverage is weakest at this point. The support of the nonshooting hand is the key to maintaining a relaxed grip and loose muscles in the arm swing.

At the end of the pushaway, the ball is extended out with both arms and with the weight of the ball still predominantly in the nonshooting hand. Movement of the arm from the shoulder has begun. The ball only needs to be pushed out as far as the nonshooting arm can naturally push it out. Once the arms are extended and the nonshooting hand begins to withdraw support, the ball should naturally begin to swing back.

Let the ball swing naturally. If the muscles of the shooting hand and arm stay loose with the nonshooting hand doing the work, the swing should develop naturally from the pushaway without a hitch. The pushaway and the swing will blend into a natural arc from the start, without hesitation and without help. At the end of the pushaway, as the nonshooting hand leaves the ball, the ball should swing following the same principles as those of a pendulum's movement (figure 4.3).

4.3 **Ball swings naturally.**

As stated earlier, a loose, natural arm swing is the key to bowling consistently, and the swing is a major part of timing. In this game of repetition, a natural swing will be the purest swing and the most repeatable. The power will come from the legs and from the momentum of the approach.

Consider the way a baseball pitcher uses his legs to throw a baseball. The motion of the legs during the wind-up of a pitch provides torque to the arm to throw the ball with more power. Similarly, a baseball batter will first step into the pitch before swinging his arms to hit the ball. Stepping with the legs provides torque through the hips to the upper body and shoulders, eventually lending power to the swing itself. Bowlers who maintain a consistent swing develop power in much the same way.

The movement of the back leg behind and over to the left side of the body at the finish generates torque through the hips, transferring power to the shoulder of the swing arm. This is how to create a powerful swing, without using the muscles of the arm itself. Developing power using the legs will be covered in later chapters.

Pushing the ball out with both hands is the key to a loose swing, allowing the ball weight and rhythm of the steps to develop the entire swing. Pushing the ball straight out, in line with the shoulder, is also important to developing a straight, accurate swing. Hold the ball in line with the shoulder. From this position, push the ball straight out to allow the ball to swing straight in the proper swing path beneath the shoulder.

A straight arm swing stays in line with the shoulder. To understand the direction of a straight arm swing, picture a clock with 12:00 directly in front and 6:00 directly behind. The head and spine are lined up directly in the center of the clock, between 12:00 and 6:00. The ball stays in line with the shoulder, which is positioned at 1:00 for the right-handed bowler. In a right-handed arm swing, the ball swings in line between approximately 1:00 and 5:00 (figure 4.4). In a left-handed arm swing, the ball swings in line between approximately 11:00 and 7:00.

Push the ball straight while keeping the swing loose to

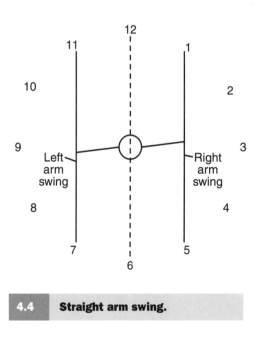

4.4　**Straight arm swing.**

keep the ball in line toward the intended target. This is the key to accuracy.

Moving Into the Back Swing The momentum that develops from a pendulum swing comes from the weight of the ball and the rhythm of the steps. With a loose swing, this momentum creates enough power for the ball to swing. The key is to create a good pushaway. Keep the muscles out of the swing and allow the ball to pick up velocity naturally.

A pure swing is a bowler's best swing. From a sound pushaway, the weight of the ball, rather than muscles, should determine the height of the back swing. With momentum and a lack of tense muscles to resist, the swing should develop naturally. A typical back swing height is from shoulder to head high (figure 4.5).

The key is to maintain the same grip pressure throughout the entire swing. The muscles of the arm should also stay relaxed, allowing the arm to swing loosely from the shoulder. This will have a pendulum effect on the ball, allowing it to swing consistently and stay on line during every shot.

The nonshooting hand needs to continue to support the weight of the ball during the entire pushaway. Pushing with ball out with only the shooting hand will cause the grip to tighten and the swing arm to tense up. This is a common trouble

4.5 **Good height on the back swing.**

spot. As the ball is pushed away, the weight must stay in the non-shooting hand so that the ball can begin to swing naturally at the end of the pushaway. Trying to support the weight of the ball with the shooting arm at this point will cause the swing to pause, and to be muscled on the way to the top of the back swing.

If the muscles used to grip the ball and the muscles of the shoulder do not remain relaxed from the end of the pushaway into the swing, the bowler may try to muscle the ball in the back swing in one of two ways: the muscles may tighten to resist the ball's swinging or the muscles may tighten to pull the swing back out of the start.

When the muscles tighten and keep the ball from naturally swinging down, they apply resistance to the swing, preventing momentum from developing. In this case, the ball will decelerate out of the pushaway on its way into the back swing. This will keep the ball from moving through a full back swing, causing a low back swing and timing problems at the delivery, because the ball will arrive at the finish before the body.

Excessive grip pressure or tense shoulder muscles that pull the swing back accelerate the back swing beyond the natural velocity of a loose swing. Forcing the momentum or pulling the ball back from the pushaway will lead to an overswing. Overswinging not only is detrimental to the swing itself but often leads to late timing problems at delivery—the ball arrives too far behind the body at the finish.

Direction of the Back Swing Tension can cause the swing to come out of alignment—the ball will not swing in a straight plane. If

you push the ball out with the muscles relaxed and let it swing, the ball will naturally move in a straight swing plane (figure 4.6). The only force that can take it out of a straight plane is muscle force because there are no outside forces, such as wind or an opponent, acting on the swing. Only muscle tension can affect the swing plane. Pushing the ball out and staying relaxed will let the arm swing as a pendulum with the ball's weight creating the momentum.

Pushing the ball in a direction other than straight forward in the pushaway can cause the arm to swing out of alignment with the shoulder. This will lead to a back swing that comes back either behind the body or away from the body, which will lead to problems in the direction of the down swing and thus lead to inaccuracy. For example, pushing the ball to the right away from the body can cause the ball to swing

4.6 **Straight swing plane.**

in toward the body, leading to a back swing that comes in behind the back. This will cause the down swing to go out to the right for a right-handed bowler.

Pushing the ball to the left toward the middle of the body will cause the ball to swing away from the body in the back swing. This will cause the down swing to come across the middle of the body to the left for a right-handed bowler.

Just Relax   How good the swing is often depends on how relaxed the arm is. To be consistent, just relax. How loose is your swing? Specifically, how loose is your arm? Starting with too much tension in the arm muscles will prevent your swing from being loose enough. To see how tense you are, extend your arm into the hand of a teammate or friend, and let that person fully support the weight of your arm so that you can fully relax. When your friend withdraws the support, does your arm naturally fall? Or is it still extended? If it falls, it is relaxed. If it is still extended, your muscles are still working!

If the muscles are tight to begin with, the tension in the arm is not conducive to just letting the ball swing out of the pushaway. While bowling, get in touch with the tension in the arm and learn to relax. Take command of the amount of tension in the arm and learn to relax to bowl better.

Arm Swing and Ball Speed   Ball speed is a product of swing speed and plays an important role in knocking down pins. Good ball speed will allow the ball to maintain its energy as it rolls down the lane; it won't burn up too much energy too soon. Some balls hit the pins weakly because they do not have enough speed at impact. Inconsistent or slow ball speed is a sign of a muscled arm swing.

A loose swing will create and maintain better speed than a tight swing. Muscles are like brakes—they provide resistance. Too much resistance inhibits the swing, and the back swing becomes too short to provide enough power in the down swing. The result is slow ball speed and less power at impact. Bowlers react to this lack of momentum by using muscle rather than proper technique to create more power in the down swing. Muscling the down swing only causes problems with timing and accuracy.

Ball speed alone is not the key ingredient to knocking down pins. Do not try to just throw the ball harder. There is a delicate balance between speed and ball roll. Professional bowlers demonstrate good speed with good roll on the ball. Using muscle to throw harder but creating less roll on the ball will not help you develop good ball speed and ball reaction. Relaxing the swing to allow the weight of the ball to develop good and natural momentum is the key to good ball speed. The proper ball weight is essential to developing a full swing. Laboring to use a ball that is too heavy only limits the height of the back swing and the momentum that it can generate to create ball speed.

Trust Is a Must   Trust yourself. Letting the ball just swing to hit a target is the goal. It is difficult for many bowlers to believe that just letting the ball swing actually works; it seems too simple to be true. The mental game becomes important because it takes trust to rely on a loose swing to hit a target. A lack of trust will cause tightening in an effort to aim the ball toward the target to control the outcome. The goal is to let it happen, to maintain a loose and consistent swing. Trying to make it happen only causes tension.

Maintain proper grip pressure throughout the entire swing. Don't increase grip pressure during the back swing or down swing. Trying to make it happen by tightening the muscles is the major cause of inaccuracy, particularly in the down swing. In a loose, straight swing that is created with the proper steps, the only force that can bring it out of alignment is the internal force of the muscles. This muscle force will keep the ball from the target. Ironically, trying to control the ball to the target will keep it from hitting the target consistently.

Sometimes adrenaline can begin to affect the muscles of the hand and arm. Various situations can cause tension in the hand and the swing. Adrenaline often will flow in the bowler who tries to continue a string of strikes or pick up a spare or who needs a shot to win the game. Controlling the effects of adrenaline, keeping it from affecting the muscles of the hand and arm, is the function of a good mental game.

Often, as a last effort to hit the target, a bowler will squeeze the ball at the release in an attempt to aim it toward the target. Keeping the swing loose enough to hit the target consistently is a better option. The most accurate bowlers in the world are the loosest.

Make no mistake, champion bowlers do feel the effects of the situation and are aware of the effect a shot will have on the outcome as well as the consequence that outcome will have on the prize. Whether it be the claim to another title or the financial implications of winning, focus requires a shift in emphasis from the outcome to the performance of the shot. Reacting to the adrenaline is the key. Controlling your emotions rather than trying to control the swing will lead to success more often.

Take it to the lane

Trying Too Hard

In the heat of competition, when you are trying to knock down the pins, it is common to try too hard to take control of the situation. Though a loose swing is actually the most naturally repeatable and consistent, squeezing the ball and tightening up the muscles of the swing in an attempt to control the outcome is a common tendency among bowlers.

Some bowlers try to hook the ball more by clenching it and only end up creating swing problems in the process. Chapter 7 clarifies how to hook a ball with leverage and the wrist. Tightening up the swing is not the way to hook a ball.

Gripping the ball harder generally leads to an unnatural back swing, creating either an overswing or an underswing. The height of the back swing is important to timing and leverage at the finish. An unnatural or inconsistent back swing will cause timing problems and affect the leverage of the body at the finish position. This in turn will lead to problems in the delivery and release.

If you swing it back too hard or too high, you will have to pull the ball back down to stay in time at delivery. This will cause an inconsistent delivery. Pulling the ball to the finish will also make it difficult to hit the target every time.

Make sure the holes are snug enough so that you do not have to squeeze the ball to hold on. Use enough bowling tape in the holes, particularly the thumb hole, to make the hole size snug (refer to chapter 1). Bowling tape is insurance for the swing!

Resisting the swing or stopping it from swinging fully will prevent momentum in the swing. This alerts the body that not enough natural power has developed. The common reaction is to tighten the muscles of the swing and grab the ball in an attempt to generate power at the delivery. This also will lead to an inconsistent and inaccurate delivery. For consistency and accuracy, rather than try harder, try better.

Give it a go

LET IT SWING

While standing still, go through the motion of pushing the ball away and letting it swing without any help or resistance. This is how to identify your most natural swing. Speeding up the swing after the pushaway is muscling the ball back; slowing the ball down to keep it from naturally swinging is tightening up the arm to control the ball. With a loose swing, you should not be able to tell when the pushaway ends and the swing begins. It is one fluid motion. Many bowlers think they have to create the height of their back swing. Actually, the combination of minimal effort, the momentum of the weight of the ball from the pushaway, and the momentum of the steps will create the back swing height. Achieving the swing through natural forces makes it the most repeatable swing. Making it swing and stopping it from swinging are the two major detriments to achieving a pure swing.

Next Frame

The arm swing is the key to consistency for three reasons: The swing delivers the ball, the swing affects the position of the hand at release, and the swing is the key to good timing. Timing is the synchronization of the feet and the swing.

The key to a good arm swing is to create a good pushaway while maintaining constant gentle grip pressure throughout the entire swing. Initially the pushaway will create momentum for the ball to swing naturally. Allowing the momentum to continue to develop by keeping the muscles of the hand, arm, and shoulder relaxed will lead to a more natural swing, better accuracy, and more consistent shots.

A good arm swing is also the key to maintaining constant ball speed with good velocity. A loose swing will cause the ball to move faster and maintain a consistent speed; a tight swing will cause the ball to lose speed. The best bowlers in the world generate good ball speed and use a strong release. A relaxed and consistent arm swing is critical to reaching your potential.

Professional bowlers bowl an average of 16 games per day during competition. The arm is not what gets tired! Stay loose and let it swing!

Timing

Timing is the coordination of the swing and the feet. Many bowlers achieve some level of consistency with a basic four- or five-step approach. A bowler who can perfect timing, however, can take her game to the next level and become even more consistent and accurate. Good timing between the swing and feet will lead to optimal leverage at delivery. Early or late timing compromises the leverage at the finish position. Late timing creates excessive leverage at delivery; early timing leads to a lack of leverage at delivery. Leverage at the foul line greatly affects both the accuracy of the shot and the smoothness of the release. Good timing throughout the approach leads to a stronger finish position and a better delivery at release.

Timing begins at the start of the swing, which is the key to a good finish. Learning to push the ball away properly is integral to a good swing and good timing. Timing will affect the finish position of the body and the delivery.

The majority of bowlers, even the best in the world, have a tendency to be either late or early. Once you understand what your tendency is, you can learn to manage it, which will lead to better scores.

Timing and Arm Swing

As covered in chapter 4, a loose arm swing is important to both consistency and accuracy. A loose swing also is critical to good timing. When the ball is pushed away at the proper time and in the proper direction, good timing will develop naturally as part of the full, natural swing.

The start of the approach is important for developing good timing. The pushaway at the beginning of the approach sets the stage for the timing of the swing. Think of the arm swing as one gear in timing and footwork as the other gear. The pushaway has a major effect on both the quality of the swing and timing.

Start the pushaway with the proper step. In a four-step approach, a right-handed bowler initiates the pushaway with the first step of the right leg. In a five-step approach, a right-handed bowler steps first with the left foot, but the pushaway doesn't occur until the second step. Pushing the right arm out with the right leg is the key to good timing in the start.

In a four-step approach, a left-handed bowler initiates the pushaway with the first step, or the left leg. In a five-step approach, a left-handed bowler's first step is with the right leg, but the swing doesn't begin until the second step. In either approach, pushing the left arm out with the left leg is the key to good timing in the start.

Good timing throughout the swing involves letting the ball swing naturally once the pushaway is complete. Don't try to swing the ball back or keep the ball from swinging. Keep the gears in sync by allowing the ball to drop into the swing naturally. Refer to chapter 4 for more on developing a natural swing.

The direction and speed of the pushaway are as important as synchronizing the pushaway with the correct step. To maintain good timing from the pushaway, you need to swing the ball to the down position with the next step (step two in a four-step approach, step three in a five-step approach), as covered in chapter 3.

The motion of the swing during the first two steps of the approach should resemble an arc or semicircle (figure 5.1). The elbows go forward during the first step and then swing down with the second step in one natural motion. As the ball swings down out of the pushaway, the arm naturally straightens from the elbow.

You should reach the top of the back swing with the next step (step three in a four-step approach, step four in a five-step approach). The top of the back swing should be neither too high nor too low. Either extreme will cause timing problems as you begin the delivery. A back swing that is approximately shoulder to head high is a good height for the back swing.

| 5.1a | Pushaway. | | 5.1b | Back swing. |

The transition from the back swing to the down swing should be natural. When the back swing reaches its highest point, the down swing will begin naturally as the last step begins (figure 5.2a). The down swing occurs as you are getting ready to begin the delivery. The delivery begins as you enter the slide (figure 5.2b). When you initiate the last step, the ball should be between shoulder and belt high in the down swing or approximately even with the middle of the back. Develop a loose swing that will fall into this zone without being excessively high. This is good timing entering the delivery.

| 5.2a | Down swing begins. | | 5.2b | Entering the slide. |

The timing of the start typically affects the timing of the finish. When the start of the approach is off, it upsets the timing of the swing and the rest of the approach. In turn, poor timing affects the finish position of the body, creating problems at delivery. Most timing problems occur in the start and surface at the delivery. Arriving either too late or too early adversely affects the body's leverage at the release.

If the pushaway occurs with the wrong step or if the ball is pushed either too far up or too far down, the timing can be impaired right from the start. The timing and shape of the pushaway are very important to finishing well.

Late Timing Late timing refers to the delay in the swing relative to the feet. The body arrives at the finish too far ahead of the ball. With late timing, the swing finishes too far behind the body. Late timing causes excessive leverage at the finish.

5.3   **Pushing the ball up.**

Delaying the pushaway is a major cause of late timing because it delays the start of the swing. Holding the ball rather than pushing it out with the first step, or the right leg (for a right-handed bowler), causes the swing to start too late. Pushing the ball too far up rather than out delays the ball's entrance into the swing (figure 5.3). Either type of start will keep the ball from getting into the down position with the next step. Starting the ball late and pushing it up are two common causes of late timing.

Assuming that the swing is loose, late timing in the start generally leads to late timing at the finish, where the body will end up at the foul line too far ahead of the ball. This will create excessive leverage at the delivery, rather than optimal leverage. You will have to pull the ball through so that it will catch up to the body at delivery. Pulling the ball in the down swing causes inaccuracy at delivery.

To improve a late start, try pushing the ball sooner to get it started with the correct leg. It might feel as if the ball is moving before the correct leg. To improve the shape of a late start, focus on moving the ball out rather than up in the pushaway.

Early Timing Early timing refers to a swing that is ahead of the feet. The body arrives at the finish too far behind the ball; the swing finishes too far ahead of the body. Early timing doesn't create enough leverage for a strong finish.

Getting the ball into the swing too quickly leads to early timing. Pushing the ball away too soon, either before the first step of the four-step approach or with the first step of a five-step approach, creates an early swing. Pushing the ball down (figure 5.4) rather than out will put the swing ahead of the feet from the start. With either start, the ball will end up past the down position with the second step. Pushing the ball away too soon and pushing it down are leading causes of early timing.

Assuming that the arm swing is loose, early timing in the start generally leads to early timing at the finish. The ball will arrive at the foul line ahead of the body. This will create a lack of leverage

5.4   **Pushing the ball down.**

at the foul line and will make it difficult for you to project the ball toward the target.

Early timing makes it nearly impossible to use the legs for power because the ball will be there before the legs can get into position to impart power in the delivery. Simply put, with early timing, you will have a lack of leverage and power at delivery.

To improve an early start, try pushing the ball later in the approach. Push the ball out with the right leg (right-handed bowler) rather than before it. It might feel as if the ball is moving after the right leg. To improve the shape of an early start, try to move the ball out rather than down in the pushaway.

Back Swing Height   The swing further affects the timing because it can create problems with the timing at the finish and affect leverage at delivery. In particular, the height of the back swing is important to good timing at the delivery.

A swing that is too high (figure 5.5) will create late timing. Simply put, an excessive swing will cause the ball to be too far behind the body when you arrive at the foul line, creating excessive leverage at the finish. A swing that is too low (figure 5.6) will cause the ball to get to the foul line too far ahead of the body, causing early timing. Refer to chapter 4 on the importance of a relaxed swing as it relates to the height of the back swing and the causes of either a high or low back swing.

| 5.5 | Swing is too high: late timing. |
| 5.6 | Swing is too low: early timing. |

Poor timing is usually caused by a poor start or a muscled swing. When the pushaway does not occur at the proper time and in the proper direction, or the swing does not develop from natural momentum, timing problems result.

Accuracy and Rhythm   At the lanes, timing problems lead to problems at the delivery because timing affects the body's position at the finish. Inaccuracy can be the result of poor timing.

Missing the target to the left from pulling the ball can be the direct result of late timing. Pulling the down swing to bring the ball back in time at the finish often leads to pulling the ball left of the target. (For a left-handed bowler, it would pull right of the target.) Pulling the ball is the most common reaction to late timing. If this keeps happening, correcting late timing can restore accuracy. Loosen up the swing and push the ball out sooner with the right leg to improve the timing of the back swing. Then it no longer will be necessary to pull the ball in the down swing to catch the ball up to the body. Fixing the late start will allow the arm to relax in the down swing and improve accuracy.

Missing the target, often to the left, also can result from early timing. The body is in too weak a position to project the ball toward the target. Missing the ball left because of poor leverage is different than missing the target to the left from pulling the ball.

Early timing will put the body in a poor position at delivery because the ball arrives at the line ahead of the body, causing excessive waist bend rather than knee bend. The shoulders end up too far forward in a position of weak leverage. This will make it difficult to project the ball toward the target and will cause inaccuracy and a weaker release.

Most bowlers have a tendency of either early or late timing. Your personality may determine in part which tendency you display. If you tend to get the swing started late, you probably like to have excessive control of the ball. If you get the swing started too quickly or early, you're somewhat out of control. Most of the time, it all goes back to fixing the pushaway and loosening the swing. But mentally, it requires an adjustment too.

A natural adjustment to rhythm goes along with adjusting timing. Do not resist it! It means that you are making a positive change toward better bowling. The swing, not the feet, controls the rhythm. Therefore, rhythm will vary, depending on the timing of the pushaway and the looseness of the arm swing. Bowlers who have the habit of a late start are naturally slower and more methodical to the foul line. When fixing timing, either by pushing the ball sooner or by pushing it out and down rather than up, you will get the ball into the swing sooner. This will be accompanied by a natural adjustment in rhythm. Getting rid of the delay will make things go faster. Loosening up the swing also allows the ball to move faster. Though initially it will feel different, do not resist the change in rhythm.

Relax! The tendency of most bowlers with late timing is to control the ball. Allowing the ball to swing naturally is one of the key adjustments to fixing late timing. Loose muscles will allow the ball to swing and get the feet to go.

Bowlers who are in the habit of starting early are faster to the foul line. Pushing early or pushing down rushes the ball into the swing. This forces the feet to chase the ball.

Many bowlers develop early timing from standing too far back on the approach. Standing too far back will give the body the feeling that it has to take off, taking steps that are bigger than natural to make up the distance to the foul line. This will cause the ball to drop into the swing too quickly and cause you to run up to the line to cover the distance of the approach. Fast feet are a classic symptom of an early start.

Moving up on the approach may be one solution to a fast approach. Fixing early timing either by pushing the ball later or pushing the ball up will delay the ball's entry into the swing. And, again, relax. Do not help the ball into the back swing in a subconscious attempt to rush the swing to stay in the comfort zone of early timing. Helping the ball back will only rush it into the swing, creating early timing. At first, adjustmenting to get the ball into the swing later, or delaying the swing, will make the feet feel slower. Mentally, stay calm and let the ball do the work.

Again, the swing controls the feet. This is why a change in how the swing moves will lead to a change in rhythm. Better timing will create better rhythm. Suddenly, when you're correcting late timing, the feet will feel as if they are moving. Correcting early timing will make the feet feel calmer and slower. Changing the start will change the rhythm, but it is a good change. Mentally, adapting to the change in both rhythm and control requires trust. Trust is a must for higher scores. Balance is the goal. Good timing and a loose swing lead to good balance.

Lane Conditions

All too often, bowlers manipulate their games, particularly the swing, to adjust to lane conditions. This often creates an inconsistent delivery when they try to make the ball do something on the lane, like delay the hook or make it hook more. For example, if the lanes are very oily and the ball does not create enough friction with the lane, a common tendency is to slow everything down to help the ball have time to hook. Bowlers usually tighten up the swing to slow the ball down, which inhibits the full swing height, which in turn affects the position of the swing compared to the body at delivery. The lack of swing height creates an early timing position entering the delivery for poor leverage at the finish.

On dry lanes, the ball might create excessive friction with the lane, and the tendency among bowlers is to force the ball down the lane. This also creates inconsistency because the muscles of the arm tighten in an attempt to force the swing to get the ball down the lane. In either case, one option is to adjust the angle or the target line on the lane, to allow for the amount of friction the ball creates on the lane. If it does not hook enough, play more directly. If it hooks too much, throw the ball to the target at more of an angle to allow it to hook back to the pocket. Another option is to use a different ball that will create the proper amount of friction to match the amount of oil on the lane, just as a golfer would use a particular club to hit the ball a certain distance. Or, adjust to the lane conditions.

Adjusting the angle or line of the shot (see chapter 8) or using a ball that creates the proper amount of friction with the lane will enable you to maintain a loose swing and good timing. That is the key to being able to produce consistent shots that score. Forcing the shot to make the ball to react in a certain way will lead to a lower average than you are capable of carrying.

LATE STARTERS

Thinking *out and down* probably will lead to a better pushaway that is not too far up. Because the tendency is to push up, overcompensating by thinking *out and down* will create more of an outward, rather than upward motion in the start (figure 5.7). You may even try holding the ball higher in the stance to create more of an out-and-down, rather than up, motion.

5.7 Think *out and down.*

5.8 Think *up and out.*

EARLY STARTERS

Thinking *up and out* probably will lead to a better pushaway that is not too far down. Because the tendency is to push down, overcompensating by thinking *up and out* will create more of an out, rather than down, motion in the start (figure 5.8). You may even try holding the ball lower in the stance to create more of an up than down motion.

51

ONE- AND TWO-STEP DRILLS

These drills will help you establish the proper swing from the start to neither delay the ball into the swing nor help the ball into the swing for proper timing. At first, practice without the ball. Once you achieve proper swing position without the ball, perform the drills with the ball to get a feel for the correct movement of the swing.

For the one-step drill, move your right arm and right leg together (out on one) as you take a step to get the feel of the timing of the start. (Left arm and left leg are together for a left-handed bowler.) Coordinating the start is the first step to good timing.

For the two-step drill, move out on one, then down on two. Stop on the second step. See if your throwing arm is in the proper position—by your side—on the second step. Repeat until the swing moves at the proper speed so that your throwing arm is down by your side on the second step. If it is past the leg, learn to slow down to get it to the leg on the second step. If the ball has not yet swung into position with the second step, get the arm to swing to let the ball down with the second step. Once you achieve proper swing position with the second step without the ball, perform the same drill with the ball to get a feel for the correct movement of the swing in the first two steps.

If you are having a problem with a late pushaway up, exaggerate the pushaway out and down on the first step (four-step approach). Delaying the ball into the swing could also be due to the direction of the pushaway. If getting the ball down with the second step is a problem caused by pushing the ball too far up in the start, exaggerate the pushaway by pushing the ball out and down rather than up with the first step.

If you are having a problem with an early pushaway down, exaggerate the pushaway out and up on the first step (four-step approach). Getting the ball into the swing too soon also could be due to the direction of the pushaway. If the ball gets ahead of the leg on the second step because you're pushing the ball down too soon in the start, try exaggerating the pushaway, pushing the ball out and up rather than down with the first step.

Next Frame

Once the ball is pushed away with the proper technique at the proper time in the proper direction, you can allow the ball to fall into the swing without force or resistance. Chapter 4 emphasized the importance of the support hand in keeping the swing arm and hand relaxed throughout the start. It can also help get the ball pushed in the proper direction. From an effective pushaway, the ball should drop into the swing in sync with the footwork throughout the rest of the approach.

To begin the approach with good timing, hold the ball in the proper stance position, push the ball away with the proper step, and push it out rather than up or down. Push it out on time, using both hands to allow the loose arm swing to begin. Keeping the grip pressure and arm muscles of the swing loose will keep the timing between the feet and the swing together throughout the entire approach.

A loose swing often can fix poor timing. Often you can accomplish this by changing the start to get the ball into the swing differently. Correcting late timing may require you to start the pushaway sooner or push the ball more down than up. Correcting early timing may require pushing the ball away later or pushing the ball more up.

With practice, you can correct your tendency to hold on to the ball too long or push the ball too late. This tendency can be strong and uncomfortable to change at first, but once you can overcome the old muscle memory and learn to create the new motion each time, the timing will be better and the effects on the swing will be noticeable. Similarly, with practice you can also correct a tendency to push the ball too soon or down too quickly by exaggerating, or overcompensating to correct the motion. Learning to make the timing later only requires practice. It will help create a position of stronger leverage at delivery. Once the motion does not feel so different, it will begin to feel better. It is just a matter of getting used to it.

Finishing Strong

Developing a strong finish position is the key to a powerful and consistent delivery To achieve this delicate balance between power and consistency, the lower body generates the power while the upper body, or arm swing, creates consistency. A strong leverage position facilitates a solid and consistent delivery.

Good body position in the finish is critical to achieving the optimal leverage to deliver the ball toward the target while imparting good rotation on the ball at release. Note that both timing and swing have a major impact on how well the body can position itself at the foul line to deliver the ball. During the approach, bad timing or a tight swing impairs the body's ability to finish in the proper position at the foul line. This will cause you to force shots, creating inconsistency and inaccuracy.

Good balance is a sign of efficiency. A lack of balance is most commonly caused by either poor timing or a muscled arm swing. Either will cause the bowler to fall off the shot rather than balance at the foul line. Good balance, an important part of the finish position, is a sign of good timing and a loose down swing.

Establishing Good Body Position

6.1 Side view.

The two views to the body in the finish position are the side view and the back view. To develop a solid finish position, you must understand it from both perspectives. With a good finish position, you are able to exercise good leverage at release while developing power throughout the delivery.

From the side view (figure 6.1), the upper body appears at the finish much as it did in the stance. The spine is tilted forward about 15 degrees so that the shoulders lean over the front knee but not much past the knee. This position is similar to the position you would get into while lifting a heavy box. The support for the object is in the legs rather than in the back.

Although the upper body at the finish is similar to the position in the stance, the body from the waist down will change. The body will finish closer to the floor through a lowering of the hips at the finish. This will enable a smooth delivery onto the lane. Lowering the body closer to the floor with the hips rather than with the shoulders through excessively bending at the waist allows you to get into a position of strong leverage at the finish, which will provide for a smooth yet powerful delivery of the ball onto the lane.

Bending both knees will bring the hips lower to get closer to the lane without compromising the upper-body position of leverage. In this position, the weight of the body is supported by the quadriceps (the thigh muscles) rather than by the lower back. This is a strong position from which to deliver the ball. The leg muscles impart force throughout the delivery while balancing the body at the finish.

From the back view (figure 6.2), the body appears in a position similar to what it was in the stance, with the exception of the right arm and right leg. The movement of the right leg is critical to the finish. Picture yourself standing in the middle of a big clock. With 12:00 above and 6:00 below, the right leg should end up around 7:30, and on the floor, for best leverage and use of the legs.

12

11

1

10

2

9

Follow through
ends up near
1:00

3

Right leg ends
up near
7:30

8

4

7

5

6

6.2 **Back view.**

On the same clock, the arm swing should follow through at 1:00. While the head remains in the middle of the body and at the center of the clock, at 12:00, the arm swings from the shoulder, which is to the side of the head, at 1:00. A consistent follow-through at 1:00 will create accuracy to the target. For a left-handed bowler, the left leg should end up around 4:30 and the left arm should follow through at 11:00.

The motion and position of the right leg serve three functions at the finish. First, sliding it over requires effort that will impart force throughout the body and to the swing at delivery. Second, clearing the leg over to the side will create room for the ball to swing beneath the shoulder at delivery. This will allow the arm swing to stay in line and finish at 1:00. Third, the finish position of the right leg behind the body and to the left side will serve to balance the body at the finish.

6.3 Side view of the follow-through.

Follow-Through A good follow-through is a sign of good momentum in the swing and will keep the swing in line toward the target after the release. A swing with a good follow-through is more powerful and more consistently accurate.

All the momentum from the loose arm swing, combined with the power generated by the legs, should lead to a good follow-through. With the hips low and the spine upright, the arm should follow through with the elbow ending up at least head high (figure 6.3). Note that the upper arm, from the shoulder to the elbow, is the arm swing, not the forearm. The arm should follow through with the muscles of the hand and forearm relaxed.

A natural follow-through at the finish allows all the momentum that was developed during the approach to keep the ball in line with the target at delivery. Facing the target with the shoulders and following through at 1:00 allow you to let the ball consistently hit the target.

From the back view, the elbow should stay in close to the head (figure 6.4). When the arm comes through, the shoulder, elbow, and wrist should end up in line throughout the follow-through. Keeping the elbow in during the follow-through should keep the swing in line, keeping the ball in line with the target at delivery. A good swing throughout the follow-through will lead to both consistency and accuracy.

Achieving optimal leverage and balance is the goal of a good finish position. While maintaining good posture is a major key in establishing a strong finish position, both timing and the arm swing affect the body's ability to achieve the proper finish position.

6.4 Back view of the follow-through.

A low follow-through is often the result of clenching the ball at the release. This inhibits the flow of momentum and ends up decelerating the swing rather than allowing it to accelerate from natural momentum.

Late Timing and the Finish Position Late timing creates excessive leverage at the foul line because the swing is so far behind the body. If you have late timing at the finish (see chapter 5), the shoulders are likely to be too far back, causing you to be too upright at the finish. When your swing is late, you have to help the ball get back in time, usually leading to a muscled down swing to get the ball to catch up to your body at the finish. Pulling the ball in the down swing is the natural reaction to late timing.

Pulling the ball creates a muscled down swing. The force of having to pull the ball through causes the hips to come up out of the shot rather than get low at the finish. This effort to pull the ball down from a late position also causes excessive force on the right side of the body and causes you to finish off balance at the line. For this reason, it is difficult to stay down with any type of knee bend at the foul line when the body is using the excessive force to pull the ball down to the release point. This is what causes the body to rise up at the foul line (figure 6.5). This will cause the right leg to rise up at the finish. Late timing and pulling the ball are common causes of a poor finish position.

6.5 Late timing, raised position.

Early Timing and the Finish Position Early timing creates poor leverage at the foul line, thus causing excessive waist bend rather than knee bend (figure 6.6). The shoulders end up too far forward in a weak leverage position as the early swing causes the ball to arrive at the foul line ahead of the body. This causes inaccuracy and weakens the release.

With early timing, the ball ends up at the foul line too soon. This causes the shoulders to lean too far forward, putting the body into a position of weak leverage at the finish and a weaker release. Early

6.6 Early timing, excessive bending at the waist.

timing often causes you to be off balance because of the early release of the ball before the legs have a chance to balance.

If your swing is ahead of your body during the approach, it is difficult for you to position the back leg at the 7:30 position because the swing will get to the finish before the body has a chance to get into position. With an early down swing, the leg does not have enough time to move over and get in position because the ball will already be past the leg and ready to release. With early timing, the right leg often stays directly behind the body in a position closer to 6:00 (figure 6.7).

When body position is compromised at the finish, the follow-through can be affected. In early timing, with the shoulders so far forward, it is difficult to finish with the arm up. With good timing and a good finish position, the arm is able to follow through with the elbow up, provided the swing is not muscled in some way.

Generating More Power With good timing and a loose swing, the body is capable of a strong finish position that uses the legs for power while maintaining a loose arm swing for consistency. If timing is good and the swing is loose, it becomes possible to develop more power by swinging the trail leg over to a position past 7:30, closer to 8:00 or even 8:30 (figure 6.8). This generates more power into the finish to naturally create a more powerful shot and a stronger release.

Generating power from the legs, while keeping the swing loose, is the natural way to create momentum without using the muscles of the

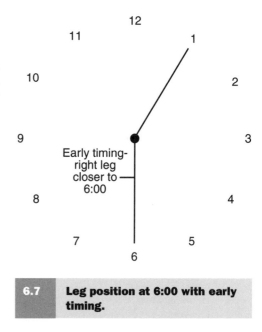

6.7 Leg position at 6:00 with early timing.

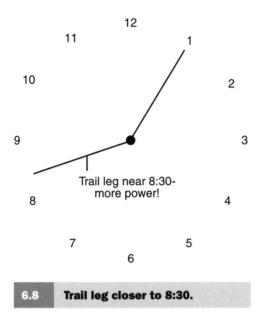

Trail leg near 8:30-
more power!

6.8   **Trail leg closer to 8:30.**

arm. If the muscles of the arm remain loose, the leg should create enough power for the swing to naturally accelerate through the finish. Forcing the ball at this point by grabbing it in an attempt to control toward the target rather than letting it go naturally is a major tendency that many bowlers have to overcome. Attempting to control the ball to the target only inhibits the follow-through and alters the path of the ball.

Clenching the ball at release inhibits the follow-through and adversely affects the ball's direction. With many of the top-level players today, you cannot tell when they release the ball by watching their swing. The thumb release is so clean that it has no effect on the flow of the swing itself, especially the follow-through.

If grabbing the ball becomes an excessive tendency after a continued effort to stop doing it, the grip or ball fit might be the source of the problem (refer to chapter 1). The follow-through should be as natural as the loose swing itself.

Missing the Target

Late timing can cause a shot to miss the target either left or right. If the body arrives at the line ahead of the ball, the ball may be delivered to the right of the target unless your reaction is to pull the ball back in time to catch it up. Pulling the down swing to bring the ball back in time at the finish often leads to missing the target to the left. Pulling the ball is the most common reaction to late timing.

Missing the target, often to the left, also can result from early timing (figure 6.9). When the ball gets to the line ahead of the body, the body is in too weak a position to project the ball toward the target.

With the right leg in a strong position, the swing can stay on its path toward the target. If the right leg stays straight back, not only will you have a lack of power but the leg also will be in the way of the swing plane. Without space cleared for the swing, you will have to swing the ball out of alignment to avoid getting hurt.

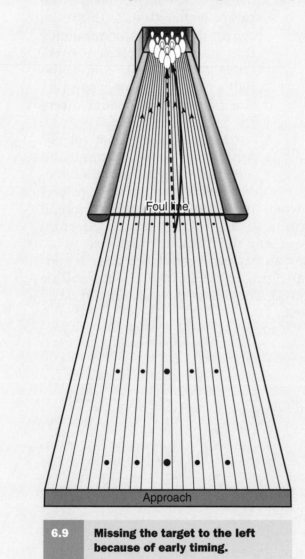

Foul line

Approach

6.9 **Missing the target to the left because of early timing.**

LEVERAGED POSITION VERSUS WEAK POSITION

Stand behind a chair that has a handle on top. Attempt to pick up the chair from two different positions. First, with the chair well in front of you, try to pick up the chair by using excessive waist bend, leaning over with the shoulders out in front of the knee. This is a position of weak leverage. Second, stand slightly closer to the chair and try to pick up the chair with the back more upright and the legs bent beneath. This is a position of strong leverage, much as you would use when picking up a heavy box.

It is difficult if not impossible to pick up the chair from the first position, but the chair feels lighter and is much easier to pick up from the second position. The same chair feels lighter or heavier depending on the position of the body. That is the difference leverage makes.

FINISH POSITION AGAINST A WALL

This drill will help you learn the feel of a strong finish position. Extend your left arm and place your left hand against a wall for balance. Put your body into a strong finish position by putting your sliding knee forward and bending it. Put your trail leg behind you and to the left. Put your swing arm in the follow-through position. Feel your weight supported by your left upper thigh. You can remove your arm from the wall to feel your body balance on the left leg.

BODY POSITION AND FOLLOW-THROUGH

To feel the difference that body position has on the follow-through, try to follow through from two different positions. First, bring the shoulder forward with excessive waist bend and bring the arm up as high as you can. Then stand with the back in an upright position and follow through as high as you can. From the first position, the follow-through is much lower than it is from the second position. As in a loose arm swing, good leverage facilitates a good follow-through.

INCREASING LEG STRENGTH

You can benefit from stronger legs because most of the power is generated by the movement of the legs and the support you provide to put the body in a position of good leverage. Exercises to build up the quadriceps, hamstrings, and calves, as well as exercises to enhance posture, such as sit-ups, will help you attain a strong, powerful finish. Bending down rather than bending over requires much more strength and is more exercise to a bowler!

Next Frame

Good timing and a loose, full arm swing are critical to achieving a strong finish position. Poor timing or a muscled swing, particularly in the down swing, will cause problems at the finish.

The goal of the approach is to achieve a solid finish position. The position at the finish determines the leverage the body has to deliver the ball. This leverage will affect accuracy, power, and the release.

With good leverage, both the delivery and the release become easier. Leverage itself delivers more power than tightening the muscles of the hand, arm, or shoulders to deliver the ball. Tightening up to help the ball at the finish, either to create more hook or force the ball to the target, may be the sign of a poor finish position that does not allow hooking the ball or hitting the target to happen naturally. This can be due to poor timing or a poor swing during the approach, leading to poor leverage at the line. Rather than muscle the ball, use the leverage of the entire body to create power and hook and to produce more powerful and more consistent shots, effortlessly.

Delivery and Hook

A solid delivery is the goal of a good approach. A proper start, natural arm swing, and solid timing all lead to good body position at the finish. Add power and momentum to the finishing body position, and it becomes the delivery. You add more momentum by sliding the foot while moving the trail leg more quickly to impart more power at the point of release. Using the legs to deliver the ball with more power will strengthen the release for more hook potential. A good delivery incorporates balance and power for strong leverage at the release point.

Sliding makes you smoother at the delivery than stepping with the last step does. Using your lead leg in this way helps you develop one fluid motion between the legs and the arm swing as you release the ball. This creates a consistent release point for better accuracy and higher scores.

While you can establish a decent average just by being accurate and picking up spares, the release is the next step to developing better pin action, both to strike more and to leave fewer pins for easier spares. Once you learn to hit the pocket consistently, learn to develop your hook shot to increase your ability to strike. The hook is the preferred method of release for getting the best drive into the pins and the best pin action on impact. All professional bowlers throw a hook to knock down more pins.

Throwing the Hook

In a sound release, the thumb exits before the fingers to create roll on the ball. A clean thumb exit is integral to a sound release. Allowing the weight of the ball to transfer to the fingers generates revolutions as the fingers impart a natural roll on the ball. Contrary to common thought, trying to lift the ball often creates excessive grip pressure, delaying the thumb release and decreasing revolutions and thereby weakening the roll imparted to the ball.

The rotation the fingers impart on the ball is determined by the rotation of the wrist once the thumb exits at the beginning of the release. Allowing the ball to swing naturally with a clean thumb release creates better accuracy and better roll at delivery. The direction the fingers rotate determines the type of release. The three basic types of releases are the straight ball, the hook, and the reverse hook (or back-up ball). Refer to chapter 2 to identify types of releases.

Most bowlers want to develop a hook at some point because a hook provides more pin action once the ball hits the pins. To develop pin action, roll the ball off the fingers to generate revolutions. The thumb exits first, and the weight of the ball naturally transfers to the fingers, imparting roll on the ball (figure 7.1). Remember, clenching the ball at release is not effective. It only delays the exit of the thumb and keeps the weight of the ball from transferring to the fingers. A delayed thumb exit creates fewer revolutions at release.

Once the ball effectively releases off the thumb and the ball weight transfers to the fingers, the way the wrist and the hand turn determines the hook. Although a hook alone isn't necessary to improve your average,

7.1a Thumb exits first.

7.1b Fingers roll the ball.

it is the preferred release. For a right-handed bowler with a hook release, the ball rotates in a counterclockwise direction (figure 7.2) into the 1-3 pocket or the right-side pocket. The hook release allows a right-handed bowler to naturally use the right-side pocket at the pins.

A hook is created by rotating the hand to the right side of the ball. A hook is a balance of two forces: forward roll and side roll. Rolling the ball off the hand from behind allows the ball to roll over more of its circumference, thus the term forward roll. Turning the hand to the side of the ball at release creates side roll. Side roll changes the ball's direction toward the pins, creating hook. The wrist and hand motion that creates an effective combination of roll and turn is the preferred method of hooking the ball.

To produce a strong hook, roll the ball from behind and then turn the hand to the side as the thumb releases. Roll from behind, then around, instead of starting on the side and turning the hand over the top. Remember, behind, then around, not around and over.

To learn to hook the ball, rotate

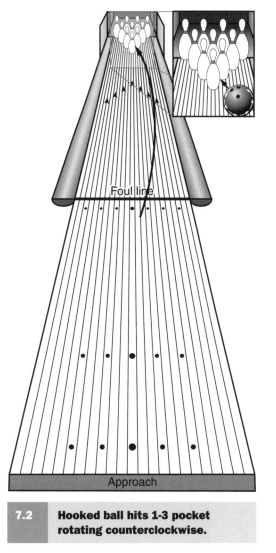

| 7.2 | **Hooked ball hits 1-3 pocket rotating counterclockwise.** |

your hand counterclockwise through the ball at release, as if shaking hands. The hand does not need to end up rotated any more than would be necessary to shake hands. One way to determine this is to consider the position of the thumb in relation to a clock around your hand.

At the beginning of the release, start with the hand behind the ball, fingers positioned at approximately 6:00. The thumb position is approximately 1:00. To hook the ball, rotate the fingers in a counterclockwise position to no more than 4:00. The fingers rotate around the thumb. The thumb should not move very much. The thumb should not pass 12:00 going in the counterclockwise direction. Just a small rotation is necessary to throw a hook.

Keep in mind that the release should not affect the follow-through. As discussed in chapter 6, the arm swing should follow through straight, while the wrist rotates the hand at the release point. A hook release is created by the motion in the wrist and hand, not the arm swing itself.

Using the Legs at Delivery   You can achieve more power at delivery if you learn to use your legs better. To tap into the strongest muscles of the body (that is, the quadriceps), you need to slide the last step of the delivery. To slide the last step, contact the floor with the toe first and transfer your body weight forward, eventually stopping as the weight comes back over the heel (figure 7.3).

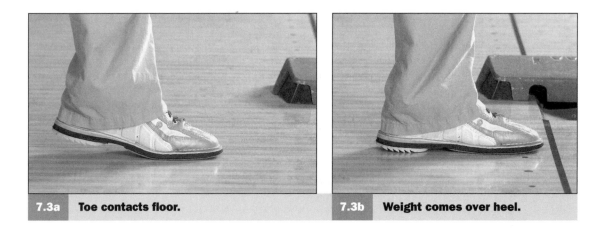

| 7.3a | Toe contacts floor. | 7.3b | Weight comes over heel. |

Sliding the last step at delivery allows the muscles of the upper leg to contribute power during the delivery. In fact, this is where the power is initiated. Sliding engages the quadriceps muscles, the most powerful muscles of the body. The power generated from the quads creates torque that will transfer to the hips, through the torso, and into the shoulder, naturally producing a stronger follow-through.

For a right-handed bowler, proper use of the right leg creates more power, enabling the arm swing to remain loose and consistent. The movement of the right leg to generate power in the delivery is similar to a baseball pitcher who generates power during the wind-up. The wind-up motion of a pitcher begins with the back leg, generating power from the right leg to transfer to the left leg, eventually transferring torque to the hips, which supplies more natural force to the arm swing at delivery.

In bowling, the equivalent use of the right leg involves sliding the right leg farther to the left of the body for more power. The right leg should end up at approximately the 8:00 to 8:30 position to generate power and clear a space for the arm to swing beneath the shoulder, balancing the body at the finish. Using the right leg in this manner generates more power in the delivery. Also, moving the right leg to the left side of the body at delivery serves three important functions: It provides space for the swing plane to remain straight beneath the shoulder, it lowers the hips for better knee bend, and it provides balance at delivery.

Powerful bowlers generate even more power from the legs, with the right leg ending up past the 8:00 position closer to 8:30 or 8:45. Extending the trail leg farther lowers the hips even farther to create more knee bend and improve the leverage of the body at the delivery. Lower hips strengthen the release.

From a Reverse Hook to a Hook Release Initially, a reverse hook comes more naturally for some bowlers. A reverse hook rotates in the opposite direction of a hook. A right-handed bowler who throws a reverse hook rotates the hand around the left side of the ball at release. For a right-handed bowler, a hook ball rotates in a counterclockwise direction, moving from right to left as it hooks on the lane. A reverse hook rotates in a clockwise direction, hooking from left to right on the lane.

A right-handed bowler who has been throwing a reverse hook and wants to develop a hook may be challenged by the opposite rotation. Staying with a reverse hook or a straight ball is an option; developing a hook may be a better option, depending on skill level. With good spare shooting, bowlers can average well into the 150s or so without a hook. Some bowlers average into the 180s with a strong reverse hook. To develop more drive into the pocket for a stronger strike shot, try developing a hook or perfecting a current hook.

The position of the hand throughout the swing has an effect on the position of the hand at the beginning of the release. If you find it difficult to rotate the ball counterclockwise for a hook, you may need to reposition the hand in the stance and throughout the swing, paying particular attention to the hand position at the top of the back swing. The hand position at the top of the back swing and during the down swing leads to the hand's position at the release point. It might be necessary to exaggerate the hand position to the right side of the ball to avoid rotating around the left side.

To exaggerate the hand position to the right side of the ball, hold the ball in the stance with the hand on the right side of the ball (figure 7.4). Keep the hand in that position throughout the entire swing. The fingers will be closer to 4:00 at the beginning of the release or more on the right side of the ball. Again, you need to exaggerate the counterclockwise rotation at the release, trying to rotate the fingers to 3:00. This will help create rotation around the right side of the ball rather than around the left side, as in a reverse hook. This is the goal when switching from a reverse hook to a hook. Exaggerating the rotation most likely will be necessary at first (figure 7.5).

Overturning the Ball Most bowlers who already have a hook generally try to overdo the rotation. Remember, a hook is a balance of two forces: forward roll and side roll. The wrist and hand motion that creates an effective combination of roll and turn is the preferred method of hooking the ball. Imparting excessive rotation makes the ball rotate on a smaller point of its circumference, creating more spin. Providing more turn than necessary only leads to excessive side roll, creating a force similar to the spin of a top. A top spins on one point and does not move much from its place. Therefore, rotating more is not necessarily better.

| 7.4 | **Position hand on the right side of the ball.** |

| 7.5 | **Exaggerate rotation at release.** |

Spin delays the ball's ability to create friction with the lane and often makes the ball slide down the lane with minimal roll or hook. Trying to hook the ball more results in more spin, which only delays the roll to the point that the ball may not pick up enough roll to hook.

Some bowlers do not rotate enough. Little rotation creates all roll on the ball, which can also appear as too little hook toward the pins. If there is not enough rotation to impart spin, there is no side roll to create a change in direction. Side roll stores enough energy for the ball to hook as it gets near the pins. Too much roll with too little rotation creates all roll and no hook. This is similar to a straight ball.

Wrist and the Release   Many bowlers either have trouble keeping their hands behind the ball or rotate their hands too soon. Others overrotate the ball at the release point. Either situation creates too much spin. Most bowlers need some type of wrist support because the wrist is a small and often weak joint. Keep the wrist firm, positioning the hand and fingers behind the ball at the beginning of the release (figure 7.6).

Wrist supports come in various sizes and lengths. Each offers a different type of support, helping to create a different type of roll on the ball. In general, many bowlers simply need some type of support to keep the wrist from bending through the swing and release. A basic wrist guard with metal on the back side of the hand that spans from the knuckles over the wrist and onto the arm strengthens your hand position to offer more support for better roll.

7.6   Firm wrist.

Release and Follow-Through   When you rotate too soon, the thumb is already past 12:00 at the release point. This often causes a second problem: the inability to create a straight follow-through. This problem often is caused by letting the elbow come out rather than keeping it in line with the shoulder and hand (figure 7.7).

Overrotating is also very common. Turning the hand past the handshake position causes much more spin than roll. It actually cuts down on the amount the ball will hook.

7.7 **Elbow out.**

In a sound release, the swing is not altered in any way. Most bowlers increase grip pressure as they get near the release in an effort to hook the ball more. They only end up spinning it and hurt the direction of the swing in the process. Maintain a loose swing with minimal grip pressure while imparting good rotation to the ball with your wrist and hand. A good balance between roll and spin to the ball is the most effective type of hook. Remember, behind, then around, vs. around, then over.

Hand Position and Accuracy   It is common for bowlers to try too hard and try to do too much when bowling. Always remember, swing is king. If you attempt a different kind of release and it creates a problem in your accuracy, go back to developing a healthy swing. Refer to chapter 4 for a reminder of how important swing mechanics are to a good delivery.

Rotating the hand too early in the swing, before the ball arrives at the release position, causes the thumb to be in the down position at the release point. It is a natural position for your hand to assume, such as when your arm naturally hangs by your side when you stand. The thumb-down position affects the direction of the follow-through, often causing you to miss the target to the left. If you miss the target to the left and it is not caused by pulling the ball, try to keep your hand more behind the ball. Focus on keeping the thumb out rather than down at the delivery.

Forcing Accuracy or Hook   Just let the ball roll off your hand as you complete a straight follow-through. Trying to aim it by using muscle as you release it only causes problems in hitting the target consistently. Trying to hit your target only causes inaccuracy. A good arm swing will be accurate and does not need help to hit the target. Learning to trust this concept is the sign of a good mental game. Accuracy is in the swing, not in the force of the hand.

Clear the Thumb Hole

Use bowling tape to get the ball to fit your hand well. (You can get bowling tape at any pro shop, sometimes at vending machines inside the bowling center.) Your thumb and fingers will fluctuate in size from many natural variables such as fluid intake, temperature, and humidity. To keep the hole sizes the same as your fingers and thumb, use tape in the hole to take up space when your hand is smaller. When your hand swells, take the tape out. Use as much tape as necessary to get the proper hole size. Even with a good-fitting ball, tape is an essential part of getting a good feel on the ball. Pay particular attention to the thumb hole so that the thumb can exit smoothly.

The idea is to keep the holes snug enough so that you do not have to clench the ball. The reason most bowlers do not exit the thumb hole cleanly is not that it is too tight, but that it is too loose! This causes the bowler to grab onto the ball and get hung up in the ball at release. Clenching a loose hole will not allow the thumb to exit smoothly.

Many bowlers try to overhook the ball, trying to "put something on it." Doing this with force not only creates inconsistency, but in many instances it also makes the ball hook less and spin more. Hook is in trusting the technique rather than in muscle force. Many bowlers think they have to do more to get it to hook. Rather than do more, do it better!

Sometimes bowlers try to put more on the ball because of oily lane conditions, or a lack of friction between the ball and the lane. If the lanes are oily and the ball is not hooking enough, consider making an adjustment on the lane (see chapter 8). It may be necessary to get a ball that creates more friction with the lane for the amount of oil on the lane. If you have a hook release, use a more aggressive ball to create more friction and increase hook.

Do not compromise fundamentals to make a ball hook. Work on technique and make adjustments. As a golfer uses a certain club for a certain distance, use the right equipment with the proper friction for the lane conditions and keep that swing loose!

STEP, STEP, STEP, SLIDE

Learn to slide by walking up to the foul line with three normal walking steps, heel to toe, then slide the last step, toe down first. Walk through this approach at least five times to get the feel of walking with the first three steps, then sliding the last step. Only the last step should be a slide step.

BALANCE AT FOUL LINE

Take note of how balanced you are at the finish. A right-handed bowler should end up with the weight balanced on the left leg and the trail leg (the right leg) behind to the left. Either the toe or the top of the foot of your trail leg may make contact with the floor for better balance and lower hips at delivery. If your trail leg has to step off to the right of your body to catch your weight at the finish, you are falling off balance. If you are off balance, something in your approach is causing it. Either your timing is off or you are pulling your swing, literally pulling yourself off balance.

LOWER HIPS

To get lower to the floor at delivery, try to make the top of the foot of your trail leg touch the floor by inverting the angle of your foot. Getting the top of your right foot (right-handed bowler) to touch the floor will naturally lower your hips, creating better knee bend in the lead leg. To accomplish this motion, the trail leg will create more power because it will have to move more quickly to achieve the motion necessary to get the foot into this position. Lower hips create a stronger release.

CLEAN THUMB EXIT

To learn to get the ball cleanly off your hand, stand at the foul line with your left leg forward, and push the ball into the swing while standing still. Once the ball gets even with your foot, bring the thumb out cleanly and roll the ball off your fingers (figure 7.8). Do this with complete momentum and a follow-through.

7.8 **Thumb exits cleanly.**

DEVELOPING A HOOK

Practice rolling the ball into some pillows or into the couch at home. Stand as if you were standing at the foul line. Let the ball swing, releasing the thumb. Make repetitive shots, developing the counter-clockwise rotation. As an alternative, you can roll the ball to a friend on the concourse behind the lanes.

PLAY CATCH

Play underhand catch with a Nerf® football to get a feel for the rotation of the hand. Try to toss a perfect spiral. You achieve the spiral by the touch off of the hand, not by clenching the ball and overturning the thumb. Notice how the rotation is in the wrist. The fingers rotate around the thumb, with minimum movement in the thumb itself.

Next Frame

Generating power from the legs while keeping the swing loose is the natural way to create momentum without using the arm muscles. If the arm muscles remain loose, the legs create enough power for the swing to accelerate naturally through the finish. Forcing the ball by grabbing it in an attempt to control it toward the target, rather than letting it go naturally, is a common tendency but only inhibits the follow-through and alters the ball's path.

The rotation of the wrist determines whether it is a reverse hook, straight ball, or hook. For some bowlers, a reverse hook comes more naturally than a hook, or vice versa. The release should never be more important than the swing itself; nor should it affect the swing, body position, or accuracy if it is properly done. That is, a sound release should not affect the flow of the swing or the follow-through. Ideally, you should not be able to tell, by looking at the swing, when the release occurred.

The strength of your release is greatly affected by the approach, particularly by the timing, arm swing, and finish position. Leverage at the finish—and all that leads up to it—affects the release. In a sound release, the thumb exits before the fingers to create roll on the ball. Squeezing does not allow the thumb to exit properly. Squeezing the ball or trying to impart "lift" only delays the thumb's exit. Maintaining the proper grip pressure to keep the hand relaxed develops a strong, effective release.

A smooth roll creates a smooth ball path on the lane rather than a jerky movement toward the pins. With a consistent ball reaction on the lane you will be able to make clear adjustments in your ball path and adjust to the lane conditions effectively.

Hitting the Pocket

For good pin action at impact, the ball should make initial contact with the pocket rather than hit the head pin straight on. The left-side pocket is between the 1 and 2 pins; the right-side pocket is between the 1 and 3 pins. Hitting the pocket is important if you want to strike. But hitting the pocket also creates better pin count on the first shot, leaving easier spares. The key to hitting the target is to adjust where you stand on the approach in relation to your target. Generally, right-handed bowlers who roll a straight or hook release use the 1-3 pocket on the right and count the boards and arrows from the right. Left-handed bowlers who roll a straight or hook release use the 1-2 pocket on the left and count the boards and arrows from the left. Bowlers who roll a reverse hook use the pocket on the opposite side and count the arrows from the opposite side of the lane because of the opposite direction of the rotation.

Adjusting the relationship between the stance position and the target changes the angle to the pocket. While adjusting this angle, consider lane oil conditions. For open bowling and recreational league play, oil is applied in a basic pattern. Oil makes the ball slide more. Generally, more oil is applied toward the middle of the lane and less toward the gutters. This knowledge is instrumental in properly adjusting the line to the pocket. Adjustments are based on how much or how little the ball is hooking. Adjusting to the amount of friction the ball creates with the lane not only will aid in proper lineup to the pocket, but it also will lead to making adjustments to stay in the pocket as the oil dissipates and the lane condition changes.

Adjusting the Angle

Determine the basic stance position and decide which target to use to direct the ball in a general area of the lane to hit the head pin (see chapter 2). At delivery, the ball is released in relation to the target in a line that, if extended to the pins, may or may not line up to produce a pocket hit (figure 8.1). This shape of the trajectory will look different for a straight ball than it will for a hook ball. The line will be more direct for a straight ball and less direct with a hook ball, to allow for the curve of the hook. The goal is to fine-tune this angle by making adjustments in the relationship between the stance and the target so that the ball will hit the pocket on every shot.

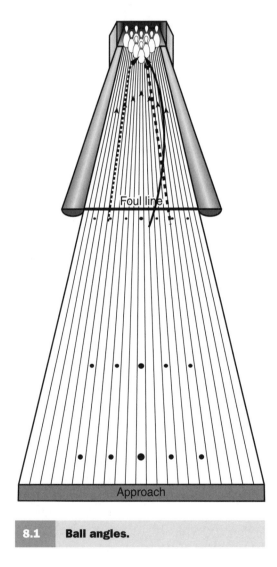

When the ball misses the pocket, the general rule is to keep the same target and move the stance in the direction of the miss. For example, if the ball misses the pocket to the right, move the stance position to the right. If the ball misses the pocket to the left, move the stance to the left. Moving the feet in either direction to change the starting position, while maintaining the same target, produces a different angle through the target toward the pins. For example, a right-handed bowler may start on the middle dot with the target between the second and third arrows. If the ball misses the pocket to the right, it does not have enough angle toward the pocket. To create more angle, move the feet to the right of the middle dot, keeping the same target (figure 8.2). Moving the feet while using the same target will change the angle of the ball path in a direction more toward the pocket.

Foul line

Approach

8.1 Ball angles.

In another example, a right-handed bowler may start on the middle dot, with the target between the second and third arrows. If the ball misses the pocket to the left, it has too much angle toward the pocket. To create less angle, move the feet to the left of the middle dot, keeping the same target (figure 8.3). This will change the angle of the ball path in a direction more toward the pocket.

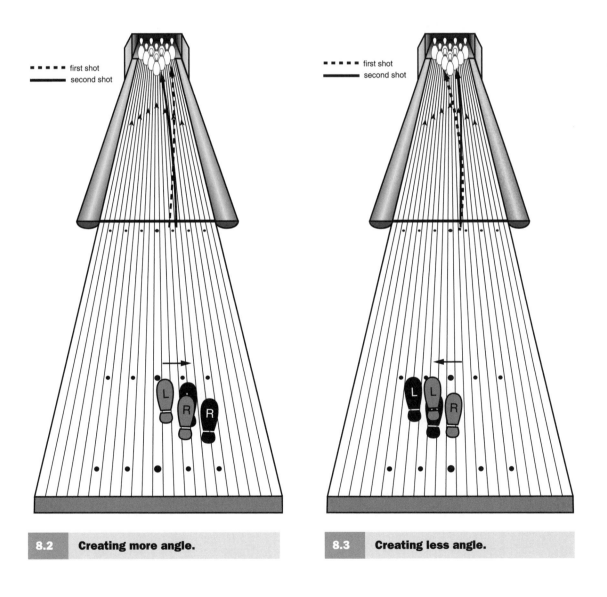

8.2   **Creating more angle.**

8.3   **Creating less angle.**

Keep in mind that the bigger the miss, the bigger the move. If the ball is not in the pocket at all, move at least three boards, if not more. If the ball impacts the pins to create either a light-pocket (solid arrow, figure 8.4) or high-pocket hit (dashed arrow, figure 8.4), make a small adjustment to fine-tune the pocket hit. In a light-pocket hit, the ball hits more of the 2 or 3 pin (depending on which pocket is used). In a high-pocket hit, the ball hits the head pin more squarely than the 2 or 3 pin.

Lane Conditions and Friction Whether the ball hits the pocket may be due to the angle of the shot or to the amount of oil on the lane. For bowlers who throw a hook, lane conditions will have an effect on the amount of friction the ball is able to create with the lane.

In the beginning of the sport, oil was applied to the lane to protect the wood. The

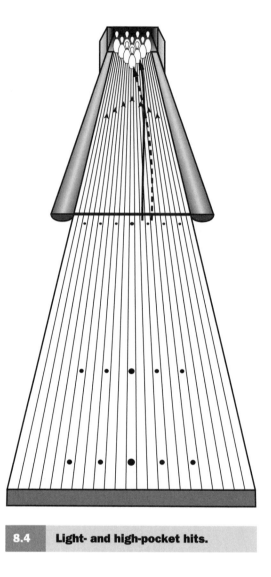

| 8.4 | **Light- and high-pocket hits.** |

oil was applied manually and served as a buffer to the friction created between the bowling ball and the wooden lane. Eventually, lane oil machines were invented to both clean and oil the lanes at a touch of a button. Bowlers discovered that the application of the oil affected scoring. The pattern of oil affected the lane conditions and could lead to higher or lower scoring. Today, lane machines are computerized, and oil application—the pattern across the lane, length of the pattern, and volume of oil—can be specifically programmed. Lengthwise, oil generally is applied around 40 feet down the lane. The lane is 60 feet, so there is some friction toward the back end near the pins.

Today's game features a basic oil pattern for open bowling and league play. A heavy volume of oil is applied toward the center of the lane; less is applied toward the gutters (figure 8.5). Where the ball is thrown on the lane determines the amount of friction the ball will create with the lane as it rolls.

Where the volume of oil increases on the lane is at the discretion of the lane maintenance personnel at the bowling center. Typically, the volume of oil increases around the second arrow on the lane. That leaves less oil outside the second arrow and more oil toward the inside, the middle of the lane. The second arrow is an approximation.

The oil line, the point at which the oil goes from light to heavy, can be right or left of the second arrow, but usually is around or slightly outside the second arrow. This has a major effect on scoring because the lane oil affects the amount of friction the ball creates with the lane. More oil makes the ball slide; less oil allows the ball to create more friction with the lane.

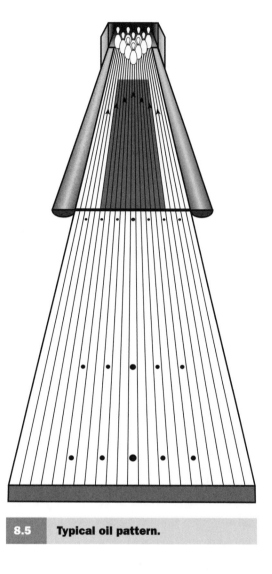

8.5   **Typical oil pattern.**

Adjusting the Hook Release to Lane Conditions   Because there is more oil toward the middle and less oil toward the outside, a bowler with a hook can modify the amount of friction the ball creates on the lane by moving the target. If the ball is sliding too much, it may be due to a heavier amount of oil toward the center of the lane. Moving the target and stance away from the heavy oil toward the lighter oil will allow the ball to create more friction (figure 8.6). Moving toward the gutter will allow the ball to roll where there is more friction.

If the ball is hooking too much, the ball is rolling on a part of the lane where there is too much friction. Moving the target into the oil provides less friction. Moving the target and stance toward the heavier oil in the middle of the lane makes the ball slide more before hooking (figure 8.7).

Again, the bigger the pocket miss, the bigger the adjustment needs to be to become flush with, or in the center of, the pocket again. Generally, the oilier the lane seems, the more direct the target line

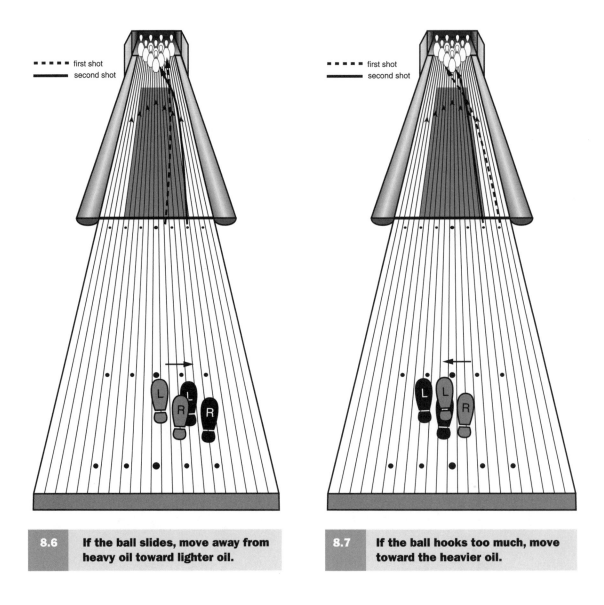

| 8.6 | If the ball slides, move away from heavy oil toward lighter oil. | 8.7 | If the ball hooks too much, move toward the heavier oil. |

you will need. If the lane hooks, then it is possible to throw the ball at an angle toward the target because the ball will hook back.

Adjust the angle of the shoulders to face the target. The angle of the shoulders sets the swing path in the direction of the target. A good swing moves perpendicular to the shoulders. To maintain that relationship, line up the shoulders so that you do not have to change the swing plane relative to the shoulders to hit the target.

Managing Friction Moving on the lane affects the amount of friction the ball can create with the lane, caused by the amount of lane oil. However, the cover of the bowling ball itself also has an effect on the ball's ability to create friction with the lane (see chapter 1).

If there is a heavy volume of oil on the lane and the angle has to become too direct to allow you to hit the pocket, it may be because the cover of the ball is not strong enough to create enough friction with the lane oil. Bowling with a more aggressive ball creates more friction with the lane. This would not require such a direct angle because the ball can grip the lane to create movement toward the pocket.

Using a ball that creates the amount of friction to enable you to play in a comfortable part of the lane may be an effective strategy to easier scoring. For example, if the second arrow is a comfortable place to play but the ball hooks too much because of a light amount of oil on that part of the lane, the ball might miss the pocket because of the excessive amount of friction between the ball and the lane. This would require a move toward the inside of the lane, perhaps more than might be comfortable. Using a less aggressive ball would not require such a big adjustment but would still allow you to play in a more comfortable part of the lane and hit the pocket.

If the second arrow is a comfortable target but the ball does not hook enough, you may be required to move toward the outside of the lane where there is less oil. Playing farther out on the lane may be uncomfortable. If so, using a more aggressive ball might be a better option. This would allow you to keep a loose swing without having to force the hook, and you would be able to play where the oil is heavier on the lane.

Take it to the lane

Keep It Natural

When the ball is not hitting the pocket, it is natural for you to have a conscious or even subconscious reaction to the amount of friction the ball creates with the lane, thus affecting your swing. That is, if the friction created by the ball is not producing the proper ball reaction and an effective path to the pocket, this will evoke a natural reaction to force the desired result. For example, if the ball is hooking too much, you might try to force it down the lane to delay the hook. This reaction of force will create a muscled arm swing. Conversely, if the ball does not hook enough, you might force the swing to create hook.

Using a ball that does not match either the friction on the lane or your comfortable angle to play affects your delivery. When the amount of friction that the ball creates on the lane does not produce the desired hook, the automatic tendency is to change the swing to try to create the desired reaction. This hinders the natural swing and often produces excessive grip pressure at release. Rather than force the ball and become erratic, adjust the angle of the shot or use a different ball that creates the proper friction to maintain a loose arm swing.

Simply put, if the ball hooks too much, forcing it down the lane impairs the natural swing. If it does not hook enough, the typical reaction is to try to put more on the ball. Whether consciously or subconsciously, most bowlers try to increase grip pressure or muscle the swing rather than properly adjust the angle or use a different ball that creates an adequate amount of friction for the lane condition. The latter will reinforce a loose swing, rather than a tight, forced swing, to actually produce the desired result.

Allowing the ball to swing naturally with a clean thumb release creates better accuracy and allows the weight of the ball to transfer to the fingers for more revolutions and a predictable roll (see chapter 7). Using a ball with the proper friction enables a loose swing and clean release.

Often it is a matter of getting out of a familiar comfort zone to play smarter. Playing smarter will relax the swing because the amount of friction between the ball and the lane will allow the swing to relax and be natural. Forcing the reaction is a major cause of a muscled swing and release.

If the ball does not hook enough, try a more aggressive ball or play where there is more friction on the lane. A more aggressive ball will grab the lane sooner, creating enough friction for the ball to roll soon enough to change directions earlier toward the pocket. Or play toward the gutter, where there is more friction on the lane. Either solution will create more friction and allow the swing to stay relaxed and produce consistent shots to score.

Some bowlers avoid playing closer to the gutter out of fear of throwing the ball into the gutter. Playing the first arrow may seem intimidating because although it seems as if it is on the gutter, keep in mind that there are players who actually target on the first board of the lane to play directly next to the gutter!

You have room to spare! Fear itself often stops bowlers from adjusting and playing another part of the lane. No matter where you are playing on the lane, the technique of using a loose arm swing should produce the same shots; it is fear of guttering that creates unnecessary tension in the swing.

Take the experiment done with a group of people asked to walk across a balance beam placed on the floor. They walked across it with ease and grace. The same people were then asked to walk across the same beam raised 30 feet and suspended in the air. (Of course, there was a platform to approach the beam and a safety net beneath.) Their ability to smoothly walk across the beam was significantly impaired. Often the people were wobbly and had to extend the arms out farther and use them to balance their awkward and tense bodies. This is a perfect example of performing the same task under a different set of circumstances that magnified the consequences of failing, which created a fear of falling. The same task was performed differently because of a different perception.

Whether you play the second arrow or the first arrow, the execution is the same. Focus on the task instead of fearing the consequences. Your comfort zone will expand, as well as your ability to score in various lane conditions!

To maintain a loose swing if the ball hooks too much, try a less aggressive ball or play where there is less friction on the lane. A less aggressive ball will slide long enough to change directions later toward the pocket. Or play toward the middle of the lane, where there is less friction. Either adjustment will create less friction while allowing the swing to stay relaxed.

Be willing to move your feet or target to change the angle toward the pocket to create a flush pocket hit. This will serve as a starting point for shooting spares, too. For half of all spares, the angle requires adjustments off the strike line to the pocket.

Give it a go

Both of these drills can help you learn to play different angles and become more comfortable standing on various places on the approach, using different targets. You may find that in either drill, you are able to hit the pocket easier from one of the arrows, or one of the dots. That may be due to the lane conditions, the type of ball you use, or your release. In bowling, there can be more than one way to score!

Learn to be comfortable standing at different places on the approach, as well as targeting at different arrows. You not always know the condition of a lane right away, but if you can adjust, you will be able to play along with the conditions, rather than fight them. Adjusting to the lane conditions and the friction that both your ball and release creates on the lane, will produce better scores. Be flexible and adjust, and you can learn to hit the pocket on every shot, for better scores!

AIM AT THE ARROWS

Practice learning to hit the pocket by aiming at different arrows. First, hit the pocket from first arrow, then from second arrow, then from 3rd arrow. To be able to hit the pocket from each given arrow, you will notice that you must adjust where you stand.

If, for example, you are trying to hit the pocket from the first arrow and your ball does not make it up to the pocket, then you (as a right-hander) will have to move your feet to the right, in the stance. This will create the angle necessary to hit the pocket from the first arrow.

If, for example, you are trying to hit the pocket from the second arrow and your ball hooks past the pocket, missing it to the left, then you will need to adjust your feet in the stance, to the left. This will adjust your angle, through the target, to create a pocket hit, from second arrow.

Make the necessary adjustments. When you first try to hit the pocket from any given arrow, you may miss. Remember, the bigger the pocket miss, the bigger your adjustment must be with your feet to adjust your angle enough to hit the pocket on the next shot.

Keep score by recording the amount of shots it takes to hit the pocket, from each arrow. To hit the pocket from three different arrows on only three shots would be perfect. To take a shot, estimating where to stand for each arrow, then taking only one shot to adjust would take six shots total. That would be excellent. Just remember, the bigger the pocket miss, the bigger the adjustment needs to be to change the angle enough to hit the pocket on the next shot.

DOT TO DOT

You can also try hitting the pocket from standing on each dot, to the right of center, on the approach. There may be two, or three dots to stand on, depending on whether the approach itself has a total of 5 or 7 dots. To hit the pocket, standing on a given dot, will require you to adjust your target to be able to adjust your angle to hit the pocket. If you miss the pocket to the left, adjust your target. This can be tricky.

If, for example, you are standing on board 15 (one dot right of center dot) and your ball does not make it to the pocket, finishing light, do you move your target to the left, or do you move it to the right?

On one hand, moving it left will create a more direct angle to the pocket; however, moving your target to the right may allow your ball to roll on the lane where there is more friction, since there is less oil applied to the lane toward the gutter. This is especially the case when you are playing around the second arrow, the part of the lane where the volume of oil tends to change, on basic lane conditions.

EQUIPMENT ADJUSTMENT

If you own more than one performance bowling ball, you may choose to make equipment adjustments, rather than angle adjustments, from any given target, or stance position. For example, if in the first drill you are playing second arrow and the ball hits light of the pocket, you can either adjust your stance position to the right to create a more direct angle, or, you could adjust by throwing a more aggressive ball to create more friction to cut through the oil and hook. This is where your creativity and comfort zones come into play. You can hit the pocket in more than one way! The one that creates enough drive to know down more pins is the better option!

Next Frame

Hitting the pocket is essential to good scoring because it creates better pin fall for more strikes and easier spares. The key to higher scores is to maintain a consistent delivery while adjusting to hit the pocket. When you miss the pocket, you need to make adjustments without forcing the swing or changing the release. Hitting the pocket after missing it completely requires a bigger adjustment than fine-tuning the ball's impact on the pocket.

To strike more, you also may need to make adjustments when hitting the pocket. When the ball hits the pocket more toward the 2 or 3 pin (depending on whether you're left- or right-handed), that is considered a light-pocket hit. When the ball hits heavy on the head pin, that is a high-pocket hit. In either case, you need to make only a slight adjustment to be able to hit the pocket flush.

Adjustments may be made with a straight ball release to adjust the angle of the shot. However, with a hook ball you need to consider the lane condition when making adjustments. If the ball is hooking too little, move to the right to find friction to allow the ball to hook, or use a stronger ball. If the ball is hooking too much, find oil to make the ball slide or use a weaker ball that slides more. A good ball reaction is the key to hitting the pocket consistently and being able to do it with a loose, rather than forced, arm swing.

Left-Side Spares

Good spare shooting is critical to good scoring. The quickest way to establish or improve an average is to learn to pick up spares. Converting or picking up an extra spare per game will add 10 pins to your average. Picking up two more spares per game will add 20 pins, and so on. Good spare shooting consists of two variables: making good shots and playing proper angles.

Spares are divided into left-side spares and right-side spares. This chapter focuses on shooting at pins that remain on the left side of the head pin for a right-handed bowler (or spares that are to the right side of the head pin for a left-handed bowler). To shoot left-side spares, note your strike angle. The strike angle will serve as the point from which to adjust the angle to knock down the pins that remain on the left side of the lane. Shooting spares cross-lane allows more room for error while allowing you to convert the spare.

To be a consistent spare shooter, have a system of changing angles so that shooting at spares is not random. A calculated system that works not only creates consistent spare making but also allows a point of reference from which to adjust if you miss the spare.

Shooting Single-Pin Spares

Single-pin spares on the left side involve the pins that are in columns to the left of the head pin. Left-side spares for a right-handed bowler include the 2 or 8 pin, the 4 pin, and the 7 pin. For a left-handed bowler, picking up spares of the 3 or 9 pin, the 6 pin, or the 10 pin would require the same technique.

Begin by identifying single-pin spares. Pins on the left side of the lane can be broken down into three columns of pins to the left of the head pin. These columns are the 2/8 pins, the 4 pin, and the 7 pin (figure 9.1). (For a left-handed bowler, identify three columns to the right of the head pin—the 3/9 pin, the 6 pin, and the 10 pin.)

Each pin is set in the same position each time, the same distance from the pocket.

Change the angle to shoot each pin based on a basic formula. To adjust for the spare, move your feet to the right in increments of approximately 3 boards per column of pins to achieve enough angle to pick up the spare (for a right-handed bowler).

Note: When making an adjustment to move the feet, look at your slide foot for reference. Take note of the part of the foot you are looking at and move that part of the foot to the proper board for the adjustment. Use the foot that ends up at the foul line. For a right-handed bowler, that is the left foot; for a left-

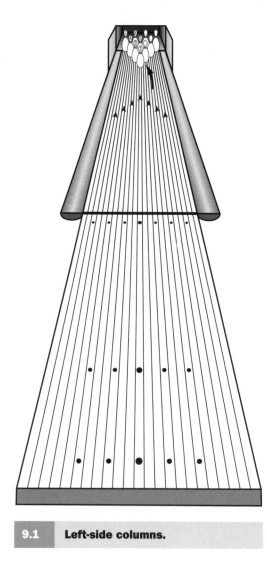

9.1 Left-side columns.

handed bowler, that is the right foot. For an effective adjustment, move your slide foot to the intended board.

For ease of reference, we will assume a right-handed bowler is shooting a spare on the left side of the lane. To a left-handed bowler, the cross-lane spare would be a right-side spare, but the technique is the same.

To shoot a spare on the left side of the lane, use the strike line as the point of reference. You will adjust your angle toward the spare from this point. Keep the same target as with the strike shot. From your strike stance position, move to the right to create enough angle to shoot cross-lane at the spare (figure 9.2).

The farther the pin is from the pocket, the more angle is necessary to shoot at it. Also consider the amount of oil in the middle of the lane. The more oil there is, the more angle is necessary to cut through the oil to get the ball across the lane. After the adjustment, turn the shoulders toward the spare to keep the swing lined up with the target line. Turning the shoulders toward the spare is referred to as closing the shoulders. Close the shoulders to create the proper angle toward the pin without changing the angle of the swing.

Keep the target the same as it was on the strike shot. Move the feet to the right from the original stance position to change the angle toward the spare.

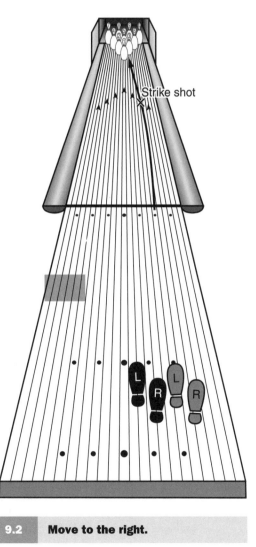

Strike shot

9.2 Move to the right.

Shooting the 2- or 8-Pin Spare

To shoot the 2- or 8-pin spare, move the feet from the strike stance position three boards to the right, keeping the same target (figure 9.3). This will change the angle of the shot to convert the 2- or 8-pin spare.

By slightly changing your angle, you can make the same physical motion as you did on your strike shot and still get the spare. Your swing should follow through the same as always, perpendicular to your shoulders. Simply turn your shoulders to adjust your swing to the target line toward the pin. Do not try to aim the ball by pulling your swing toward the middle of your body, because that would be counterproductive to your adjustment. Just trust yourself, follow through straight, and let the angle do all the work!

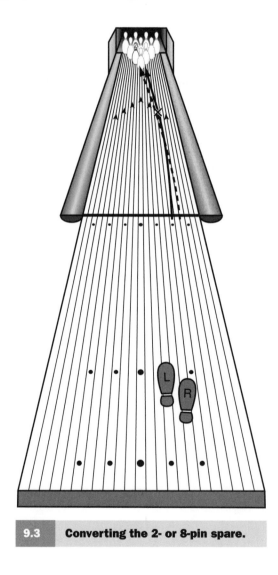

9.3 Converting the 2- or 8-pin spare.

Shooting the 4-Pin Spare

To shoot the 4 pin, move six boards to the right from the original strike position and keep the same target (figure 9.4). Moving six boards will change the angle of the shot through the strike target to allow enough angle to convert the 4-pin spare.

Again, be sure to close the shoulders toward the 4 pin to naturally line up your swing plane to the intended target line rather than force your swing across your body to force the ball cross-lane. Too many bowlers try to force the ball to the pin rather than make the same strike shot motion on a different angle on the lane. Trust is a must!

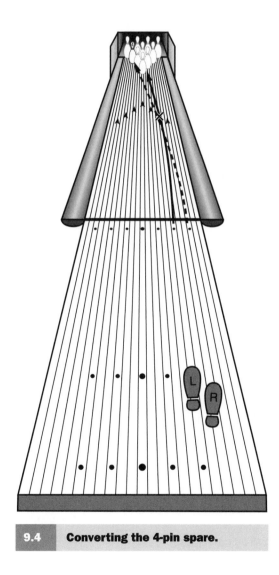

9.4   **Converting the 4-pin spare.**

Shooting the 7-Pin Spare

To shoot the 7 pin, move nine boards to the right of the strike stance position, keeping the same strike target (figure 9.5). Converting the 7-pin spare requires the largest change in angle because the 7 pin is the farthest left on the lane, requiring you to adjust and stand the farthest right on the approach.

Close your shoulders toward the 7 pin. This is the most closed the shoulders will ever need to be. Standing with the shoulders so closed in the stance may compel you to pull your swing across your body even more. Continue to trust the angle set by your shoulders and follow through straight.

When you're shooting at spares, the goal is to change the angle enough so that you do not have to alter the shot, particularly the swing. The arm swing should always be perpendicular to the shoulders. That is, the swing plane should be at a 90-degree angle from the shoulders from start to finish.

To change the angle of the shot without compromising the swing plane, adjust the feet to create a better angle toward the spare. Then turn the shoulders (that is, close them) enough to keep the swing plane on the new target line. This creates the proper angle toward the pin without changing the angle of the swing.

Closing the shoulders is done by feel; it is not an exact science. Just a slight move will allow the swing to stay on the intended target line without changing the swing in any way. You can accomplish the total angle adjustment by moving the feet to the right far enough to create an angle toward the spare.

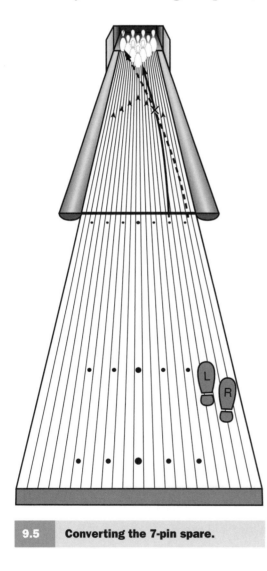

9.5   **Converting the 7-pin spare.**

Multiple-Pin Spares

While single-pin spares may remain on the deck after you throw a strike shot, there will be many occasions when multiple pins remain on the deck. Part of the process to increase your average is to hit the pocket more consistently and leave spares with fewer pins. The key to making an adjustment for multiple-pin spares is to identify the key pin (the pin closest to you) and make the appropriate adjustment for that pin. For example, for any multiple-pin spare with the 2-pin as the key pin, the basic adjustment will be approximately three boards to the right. Common spares with 2 pin as the key pin include the 2-4, 2-5, 2-8, 2-4-5, 2-4-8, and 2-4-5-8.

To convert the 2-pin combinations that include 3 pins or more, such as the 2-4-5, 2-4-5-8, or 2-4-8 combinations, move three boards to the right. This allows the ball to contact the pins just right of the 2 pin. The ball will hit the 2 pin on the right, then hit the 5 pin (if it is there); the 2 pin will hit the 4 and 8 pins (figure 9.6).

In all cases, the ball should contact the right side of the 2 pin, requiring a three-board adjustment from the strike line. With a good shot, if that adjustment does not convert the spare, then move either more or less the next time to adjust the angle to convert the spare. For example, if you move three boards to the right and the ball does not have enough angle, and you leave the 4 pin, move an extra board to the right the next time. If the ball crosses over the 2 pin and you leave the 5 pin standing, move less, perhaps two boards, the next time to decrease your angle toward the spare.

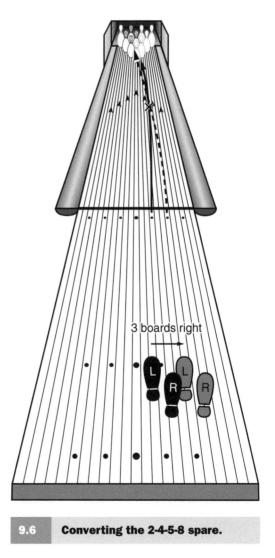

3 boards right

9.6   **Converting the 2-4-5-8 spare.**

Other spares that include the 2 pin are the 2-4, 2-5, and 2-8. While the basic move starts with a three-board adjustment off the strike line, the 2-4 spare can be converted a higher percentage of the time when the ball strikes both pins. To fine-tune the angle for the 2-4 spare, make an adjustment that compromises the angle between shooting either pin as a single pin. For example, if you move three boards to shoot the single 2 pin and six boards to convert the single 4 pin, move three to six boards for the ball to strike both pins of the 2-4 spare.

When converting a 4-pin combination, such as the 4-7 (figure 9.7), adjust approximately six boards to the right, but be sure to allow the ball to hit both pins for a better conversion percentage. This is particularly effective for spares with only two pins next to each other. To figure the adjustment for this spare, simply figure out the number of boards to move for either pin and split the difference. For example, the adjustment for the single 4 pin would be six boards; the adjustment for the single 7 pin would be nine boards. For the ball to contact both, split the difference. Make a seven- or eight-board adjustment. This will be the most successful adjustment to convert the 4-7 spare.

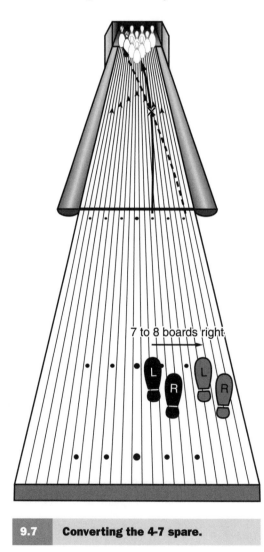

7 to 8 boards right

Just for Left-Handed Bowlers

To a left-handed bowler, a right-side spare requires a technique similar to that of a right-handed bowler's left-side spare. A right-side spare requires a left-handed bowler to bowl across the lane to where the pins are.

Single-Pin Spares

Start out by identifying right-side single-pin spares. Pins on the right side of the lane can be divided into three columns of pins to the right of the head pin. These columns can be identified as the 3 and 9 pins, the 6 pin, and the 10 pin (figure 9.8). Each pin is set in the same position each time and the same distance from the pocket. Change the angle to shoot each pin, based on a simple formula: Move approximately three boards to the left per column of pins.

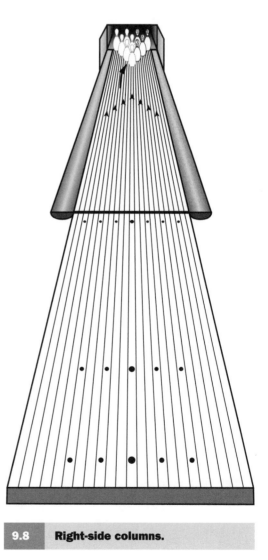

9.8   **Right-side columns.**

Keep the target the same as it was on the strike shot and move the feet to the left from the original stance position to change the angle toward the spare. For example, to shoot the 3- or 9-pin spare, move the feet three boards to the left of the strike stance position, keeping the same target (figure 9.9). This will change the angle of the shot to convert the 3- or 9-pin spare.

To shoot the 6-pin spare, move six boards to the left of the original strike stance position (figure 9.10). Keep the same target as you'd use with the strike shot. Moving the feet six boards will change the angle of the shot through the strike target to allow enough angle to convert the 6-pin spare.

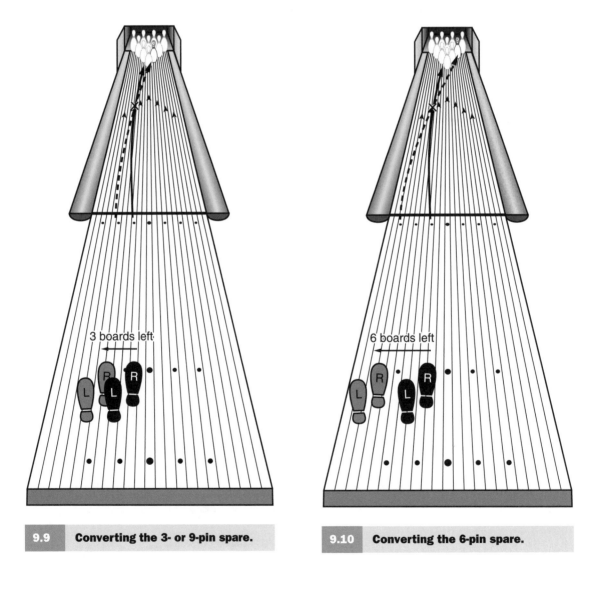

9.9   **Converting the 3- or 9-pin spare.**

9.10   **Converting the 6-pin spare.**

To shoot the 10-pin spare, move nine boards to the left, keeping the same strike target (figure 9.11). The 10-pin spare shot requires the most angle change because the 10 pin is the farthest to the right, requiring you to adjust and stand the most left on the approach.

As stated previously, the goal is to change the angle enough to avoid altering the shot, particularly the swing. The arm swing should always be perpendicular to the shoulders. The swing plane should be at a 90-degree angle from the shoulders, start to finish. To change the angle of the shot without compromising the swing plane, adjust the feet to create a better angle toward the spare. Close the shoulders to keep the swing plane on the new target line.

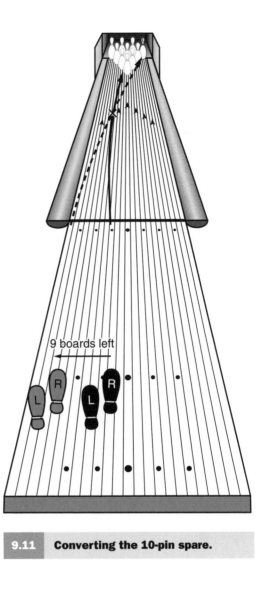

9.11 Converting the 10-pin spare.

Multiple-Pin Spares

For any multiple-pin spare, including the 3 pin, the basic adjustment will be approximately three boards. Many spares include the 3 pin.

To convert the 3-5-6 pin combination, the basic adjustment is to move three boards to the left, allowing the ball to contact the pins just left of the 3 pin (figure 9.12). The ball will hit the 3 pin on the left, then hit the 5 pin. The 3 pin will take out the 6 pin.

Similar spares will be the 3-5-6-9, the 3-6-9, and the 3-9. In all cases, the ball should contact the left side of the 3 pin, requiring an adjustment of approximately three boards from the strike line.

After leaving a 6-pin combination, such as the 6-10 spare, you need to adjust approximately six boards to the left, but adjust this number to allow the ball to hit both pins for a higher-percentage conversion. To figure the adjustment for the 6-10 spare, simply figure out the number of boards to move for either pin and split the difference. The adjustment for the single 6-pin spare would be six boards; the adjustment for the single 10-pin spare would be nine boards. For the ball to contact both, split the difference (figure 9.13). Moving seven to eight boards will prove the most successful adjustment to convert the 6-10 spare, most of the time.

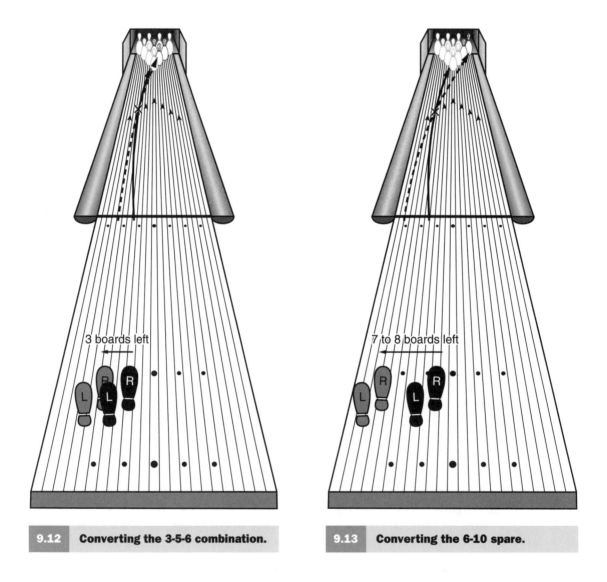

9.12 **Converting the 3-5-6 combination.**

9.13 **Converting the 6-10 spare.**

Identify Spare, Adjust Angle, and Make a Good Shot

After the first shot, learn to identify which pins are left standing on the lane. Knowing which pins are standing will allow you to identify the key pin to the spare. The key pin is the pin that is closest to you, the one standing in front of the others. Once you know which pin is the key pin, you can move the appropriate number of boards to convert the spare.

Take the time to count the boards to adjust the angle properly. You can do this while waiting for the ball to return from the first shot. A lot of bowlers think that professionals don't take the time to count the boards for spares, but in fact, the really good spare shooters always take the time to do so, either on the approach or while waiting for the ball to come back. One you have taken the time to engineer your adjustment, take your stance on the approach and adjust the shoulders to set the swing in the direction of the spare. The approach for the spare shot should be the same as the approach for the strike shot. The arm swing should not know the difference.

To adjust the angle, move the appropriate number of boards, adjust the shoulders to create the proper direction for the swing, and approach the line the same way as you would for the strike shot. Proper adjustment and good shoulder angle are the keys to making any spare consistently.

Adjust the angles more or less depending on lane conditions. If the lanes are oilier, move over to the right more to cut through the oil better. More oil means less friction for the ball to hook. If the lanes are drier and there is more friction, move less to the right when shooting spares on the left side to allow for the amount the ball might hook.

Finally, make a good shot! If you make a good shot but do not pick up the spare, figure out how to adjust the next time. Making a good shot will enable you to either pick up the spare or, if you miss it, determine how you need to adjust the angle the next time to make the spare.

Give it a go

Pin Recognition

Part of adjusting to a spare is accurately identifying the pins that are remaining. Obtain or create various illustrations of combinations of pins that may remain to the left side of the head pin. Identify the pins. At the bowling center, compare the pins remaining to your diagram.

Spare Shooting Process

To practice shooting spares, choose a pin or pins out of a full rack of pins to shoot at, as if you left that spare. Then identify the target (strike target for left-side spares). Next, adjust the angle. Decide how many boards to adjust for the spare from the stance position on the first shot. Count the boards to the right, then put your foot in the proper stance position to shoot the spare. Adjust your shoulders. Close your shoulders to the spare. Finally, make a good shot. A good shot will either pick up the spare or lead you to the proper adjustment in angle to pick it up the next time you leave it.

Next Frame

A good spare shooting system gives you the proper adjustments in angle to create room for error toward the pins so that you're able to convert spares consistently. The more angle you have, the more room for error at the target to be able to convert the spare. For cross-lane spares, the farther the spare is to the left, the more you'll need to adjust to the right.

Shooting cross-lane creates more room for error than shooting straight at the spare directly down the lane. This will lead to an increased percentage of spare conversions without requiring you to be perfectly accurate. Of course, multiple-pin spares are more difficult to convert than single-pin spares. With angle in your favor, even if you miss the target you're more likely to convert the spare.

With a good spare shooting system, you can easily make adjustments to convert a missed spare, based on a calculated system of shooting at the pins. If you make a logical move to convert a spare and you miss the spare, then you can adjust to create a bigger or smaller angle to convert the spare the next time. By simply moving to change the angle to compensate for the miss, spares can become routine rather than guesswork.

Make the adjustments to pick up all the spares to the left of the head pin (for right-handers) from your strike line. Use the strike target and move the feet, incrementally, from the stance position of the strike shot. Right-handers move right; left-handers move left. Next, using a target toward the center of the lane to shoot at spares to the right of the head pin (to the left side of the head pin for left-handers) requires adjustments from the corner pin shot, to be determined in chapter 10.

Remember, good spare shooting is the key to establishing a higher average.

Right-Side Spares

The quickest way to improve an average is to pick up more spares. This chapter focuses on converting right-side spares (that is, pins remaining to the right of the head pin for a right-handed bowler). The same techniques would be used for a left-handed bowler shooting a left-side spare, in which pins remain to the left of the head pin.

The cross-lane theory of spare shooting—enabling you to shoot at and pick up spares—applies to right-side spares as well. You can pick up right-side spares from the left side of the lane to create more accurate and consistent conversions.

Whereas the strike stance position and target determine the point from which you adjust for the spares on the left, the corner pin shot will provide the point of reference for spares on the right. The corner pin for a right-handed bowler is the 10 pin; for the left-handed bowler, the 7 pin. For right-side spares, use a target between the third and fourth arrows. Because the point of origin from which to adjust for right-side spares will be the corner pin shot, start by determining the angle to use for shooting the 10 pin, then work back through the rack to the 6 pin, then the 3 and 9 pins. You can target between the third and fourth arrows for all spares on the right side.

Many bowlers think that picking up the corner pin on the opposite side of the lane is difficult to do, or they just accept a mental block as the problem. It is not difficult, nor does it have to be a mental challenge, if you know what to do. Once you determine the best angle to use for picking up the spare, it will serve as the origin from which to adjust to shoot the other right-side spares.

Some bowlers who throw a hook have problems hitting the corner pin if they use a ball that creates too much friction on the lane. An aggressive ball will tend to hook away from the corner pin at the last second, which will make it more challenging to pick up the spare. Using a different ball, one with a a plastic cover, is a great solution to this problem.

Shooting Single-Pin Spares

Single-pin spares to the right side of the head pin include the 3 or 9 pin, the 6 pin, and the 10 pin (figure 10.1). Right-side spares for a left-handed bowler include the 2 or 8 pin, the 4 pin, and the 7 pin.

For ease of reference, instructions are given for a right-handed bowler. Left-handed bowlers can refer to the section later in this chapter.

To shoot a spare on the right side of the lane, start with the corner pin shot. First, determine the optimal angle to use for shooting at the 10 pin by standing to the far left and aiming between the third and fourth arrows to achieve the best angle, cross-lane, toward the corner pin. Again, right-handers count the arrows from the right; left-handers count from the left. The exception is a reverse hook bowler, who would identify with the bowler using the opposite hand.

Once you determine the corner pin shot, the adjustment for the remaining spares is to move to the right, from the 10-pin position in the stance, in three-board increments to convert pins in the remaining columns based on their relation to the 10 pin.

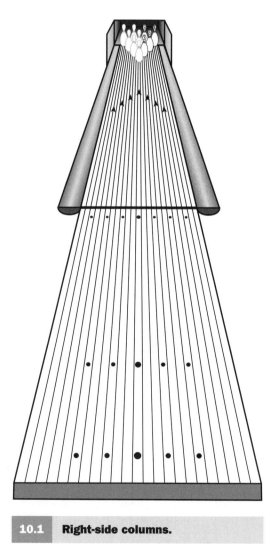

10.1 **Right-side columns.**

Converting the 10-Pin Spare

For a right-handed bowler, the 10 pin is the corner pin (figure 10.2). The corner-pin shot, or 10-pin shot, will serve as the point of reference for all other spares on the right side of the lane. To adjust for the other spares on the right side, determine an optimal angle for shooting the 10 pin to make effective adjustments for consistent success in converting these spares.

Determine the optimal angle from the left side of the lane for shooting the corner pin. The optimal angle is the most forgiving angle for shooting the 10 pin, providing the most room for error at the target to still convert the spare. To shoot the 10 pin with the optimal angle, stand approximately on board 35 on the far-left side of the lane. Use a target between the third and fourth arrows (figure 10.3). To throw

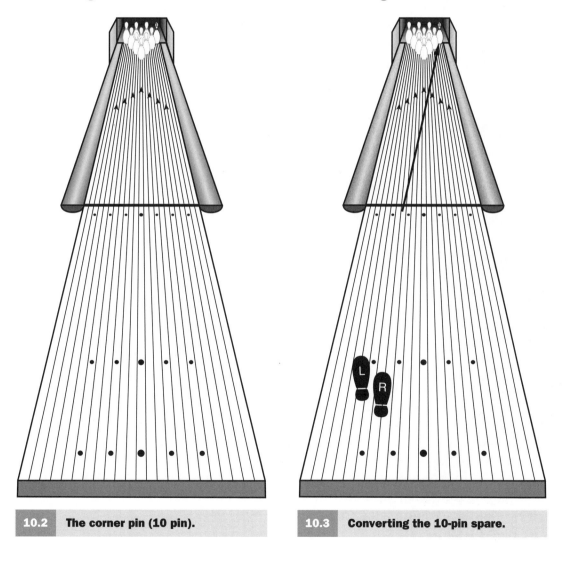

10.2 The corner pin (10 pin).

10.3 Converting the 10-pin spare.

the ball on an angle toward the 10 pin, open the shoulders toward the 10 pin. This is the key to maintaining a consistent swing plane perpendicular to the shoulders.

This angle toward the corner pin, with the target between the third and fourth arrows, is optimal from the stance position on approximately board 35. Remember to line up with your slide foot. Maintain this angle at delivery while approaching the foul line. To do this, walk straight, ending up on the same board at the finish as in the stance.

Again, start on approximately board 35, use a target between the third and fourth arrows, and walk straight with open shoulders to convert the 10-pin spare consistently. The angle toward the corner pin can be modified from board 35, depending on your release and the success of the shot to pick up the 10 pin. Some bowlers stand closer to board 33, some on board 38. Stand where you will have the most success. Board 35 is a good starting point. This shot serves as the point of reference for other spares on the right side of the lane. The target for all spares on the right will be between the third and fourth arrows.

10.4   **Shoulders in open position.**

To adjust the angle for other right-side spares, use the 10-pin target line as the reference point. The rest of the pins on the right side of the lane can be broken down into two columns in their relation to the 10 pin: the 6 pin and the 3 and 9 pins.

Note: The adjustment for these pins is not made from their relation to the head pin; rather, the adjustment is made from their relation to the 10 pin. Keeping the same target as you had for the 10 pin (between the third and fourth arrows), change the angle by moving the feet approximately three boards to the right from the stance position for the 10 pin per column of pins as they are positioned from the 10 pin. To convert these spares, turn the shoulders to an open position to keep the swing lined up with the target (figure 10.4). For a right-hander in an open-shoulder position, the right shoulder is behind the left shoulder in the stance, to face the spare on the right.

Converting the 6-Pin Spare

Keep the same target, between the third and fourth arrows. From the stance position for the corner shot, move the feet to the right to change the angle toward the 6 pin. To shoot the 6 pin, which is next to the corner pin, move the feet three boards to the right from the stance position for the 10 pin (figure 10.5). By keeping the same target and moving the feet to the right, you will change the angle of the shot, from the 10-pin shot, to convert the 6-pin spare.

Converting the 3- or 9-Pin Spare

To shoot the 3 or 9 pins, which are in the same column, move six boards to the right of the original 10-pin stance position (figure 10.6).

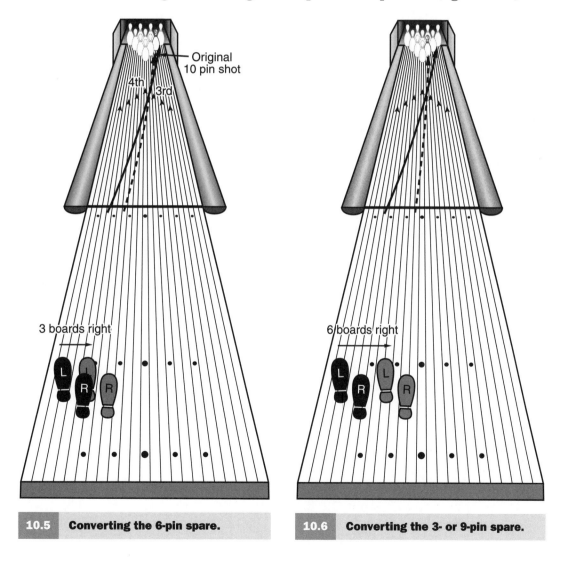

10.5	Converting the 6-pin spare.

10.6	Converting the 3- or 9-pin spare.

Keep the target between the third and fourth arrows. Moving the feet six boards changes the angle of the shot through the 10-pin target, providing the proper angle to convert the 3- or 9-pin spare.

Converting Consistent Spares

There is not a nine-board adjustment for converting right-side spares, because that would bring you back to the head pin. Beginning with the 10-pin shot, there are only two basic adjustments to convert other right-side single-pin spares, because the 10 pin shot was the original cross-lane shot for this side.

Again, the goal is to change the angle enough to avoid altering the swing. To shoot cross-lane and maintain an arm swing that is perpendicular to the shoulders, keep the shoulders in an open position toward the spare. The swing plane should remain at a 90-degree angle from the shoulders from start to finish. Adjusting the shoulder angle for each shot is the key to maintaining a consistent arm swing to convert each spare.

Multiple-Pin Spares

Multiple-pin spares on the right side include spares with the 3 pin as the key pin. Common combinations with the 3 pin as the key pin include the 3-6, 3-9, 3-6-10, 3-6-9-10, and 3-10.

In shooting the 3-6, 3-6-10, and the 3-10 (commonly referred to as the baby split), the goal is the same: to put the ball between the 3 and 6 pin (even in the case of the 3-10 split, when the 6 pin is missing). All three spares are the same as shooting the 3-6 spare. To make the proper adjustment, refer to the adjustments for shooting both the 3 pin and 6 pin as single-pin spares. Then, move to a position between the two adjustments so that the ball makes contact with both pins, in between the 3- and 6-pin positions. For example, to convert the 3-6 spare, figure the adjustments made for either pin as a single pin. Keeping the target between the third and fourth arrows, when leaving the 6 pin, the adjustment is to move three boards right from the 10-pin position. The adjustment for the 3 pin is to move six boards right. For the ball to hit in between both pins, make an adjustment of four or five boards (4.5 boards) to pick up the 3-6 pin combinations (figure 10.7).

Other spares that include the 3 pin are the 3-9 and the 3-6-9-10. These spares require that the ball contact the 3 pin more squarely, or even slightly to the left, to convert them. To make an adjustment for these spares, move to the right more than you would for the 3-

6 pin combinations covered earlier. These spares are more difficult and require more precision in angle. To attempt these spares, start by moving approximately seven to eight boards to the right, from the 10-pin position. If you miss the spare, modify this angle when you leave the spare again. Move your feet more or less, to make the proper adjustment in angle. A system of counting boards to make an adjustment allows you to revise your adjustment, based on the success of the angle, as you attempt to pick up the spare again.

Other common spares, with the 6 pin as the key pin, include the 6-10 and 6-9-10. In either case, the goal is to put the ball between the 6 and 10 pins. Therefore, both spares are equivalent to shooting the 6-10 spare.

To convert the 6-10 combination (figure 10.8), stand between the 10 pin and 6 pin position. If you start on board 35 to shoot the 10

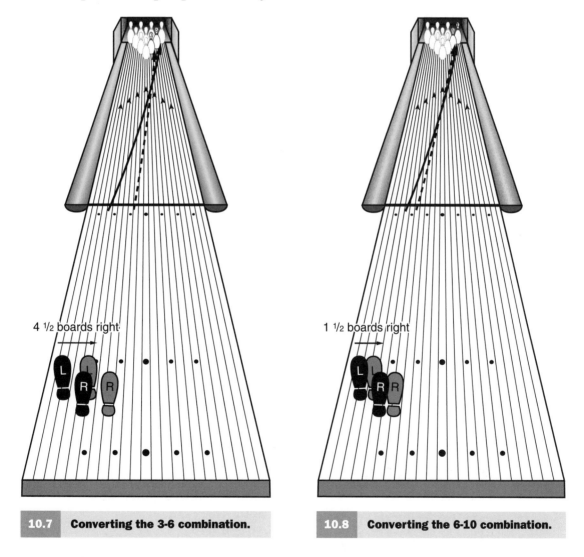

4 1/2 boards right

1 1/2 boards right

| 10.7 | Converting the 3-6 combination. |

| 10.8 | Converting the 6-10 combination. |

pin and adjust three boards to the right to shoot the 6 pin, then the adjustment to shoot the 6-10 would be 1.5 boards to the right from the 10-pin position. This allows the ball to contact both pins for a higher percentage of conversion. If, for example, you stood on 35 to shoot the 10 pin and 32 to shoot the 6 pin, you would stand on board 33.5 to shoot the 6-10 combination.

Just for Left-Handed Bowlers

A left-handed bowler's left-side spare requires a technique similar to a right-handed bowler's right-side spare; that is, the left-handed bowler needs to shoot the left-side spares from the right side of the approach.

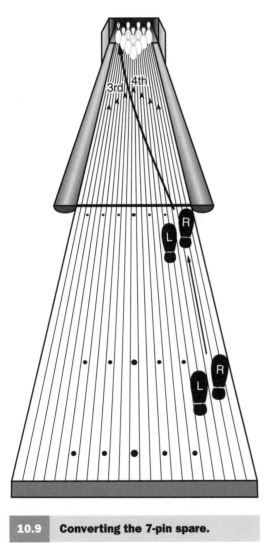

Single-Pin Spares

To a left-handed bowler, the corner pin is the 7 pin. The 7-pin shot serves as the point of reference for other spares on the left side of the lane. To adjust for other spares on the left side, determine an optimal angle for shooting the 7 pin.

The optimal angle is the angle that provides the most room for error when shooting at the 7 pin. To shoot the 7 pin with the optimal angle, stand approximately on board 35 on the far-right side of the lane (figure 10.9). Use a target between the third and fourth arrows. To throw the ball at an angle toward the 7 pin, open the shoulders toward the 7 pin. For the left-hander, this means bringing the left shoulder back in the stance, behind the right shoulder, to face the 7 pin. This is the key to maintaining a consistent swing plane in line with the target line and perpendicular to the shoulders.

10.9 Converting the 7-pin spare.

This angle toward the corner pin is optimal. Maintain this angle at delivery as you approach the foul line. Walk straight, ending up on the same board at the finish as you started on in the stance.

Start approximately on board 35, use a target between the third and fourth arrows, and walk straight with open shoulders. This is the easiest way to convert the 7-pin spare consistently. This shot serves as the point of reference for all other left-side spares. The target for all left-side spares is between the third and fourth arrows.

To adjust the angle for other left-side spares, use the 7-pin shot as a reference. The rest of the pins on the left side of the lane can be broken down into two columns: the 4 pin and the 2 and 8 pins. Keep the same target as the 7-pin spare and change the angle with the feet, based on a simple formula.

Keep the target the same as it was on the corner-pin shot. To change the angle, move the feet to the left from the original stance position for the corner pin. For example, to shoot the 4 pin, which is next to the 7 pin, move the feet three boards to the left of the stance position for the 7 pin (figure 10.10). Keep the same target (between the third and fourth arrows). This will change the angle of the shot to convert the 4-pin spare.

To shoot the 2 or 8 pins, which are in the same column, move six boards to the left of the original 7-pin stance position (figure 10.11). Keep the target between the third and fourth arrows. Moving the feet six boards changes the angle of the shot through the 7-pin target, providing a proper angle for converting the 2- or 8-pin spare.

There is not a nine-board adjustment for left-side spares, because that would bring you back to the head pin. Beginning with the 7-pin shot, there are two basic adjustments to convert the other left-side single-pin spares.

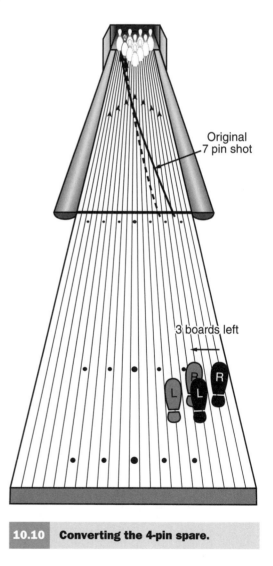

Original 7 pin shot

3 boards left

10.10 Converting the 4-pin spare.

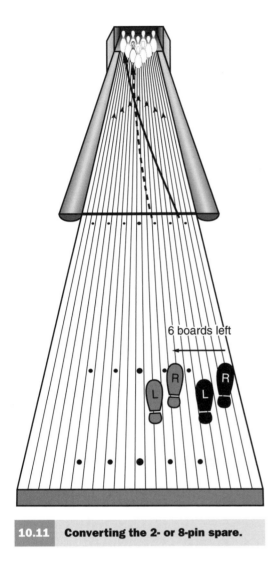

6 boards left

10.11 **Converting the 2- or 8-pin spare.**

Again, the goal is to change the angle enough to avoid altering the swing. The arm swing should remain perpendicular to the shoulders. The swing plane should remain at a 90-degree angle from the shoulders from start to finish. Adjusting the shoulder angle for each shot is the key to maintaining a consistent arm swing to convert each spare.

To change the angle of the shot without compromising the swing plane, adjust the feet to create a better angle toward the spare. Turn the shoulders toward the target line. This will set the swing plane in the proper direction. As explained in chapter 9, turning the shoulders toward the left-side spare is referred to as opening the shoulders. This creates the proper angle toward the pin without changing the swing.

Multiple-Pin Spares

Single-pin spares may remain on the deck after you throw a strike shot, but you also will have many occasions in which multiple pins remain on the deck. For example, a left-handed bowler might leave both the 4 pin and the 7 pin.

To convert the 4-7 combination, stand in a position between the 7 and 4 pin (figure 10.12). If you start on board 35 to shoot the 7 pin and the adjustment to shoot the 4-pin single-pin spare is three boards to the left, then the adjustment to shoot the 4-7 would be 1.5 boards to the left from the 7-pin position. This allows the ball to contact both pins for a higher percentage of conversion.

To convert spares including the 2-4 combination, the basic adjustment is to move between the adjustment made for either the 2- or 4-pin single-pin spare (figure 10.13). Because the highest percentage of spare conversion happens when the ball contacts both pins, the goal is to have the ball hit between the 2 and 4 pins. If the adjustment to convert the 4-pin spare is to move three boards to the left from the corner-pin position and the adjustment to convert the 2-pin

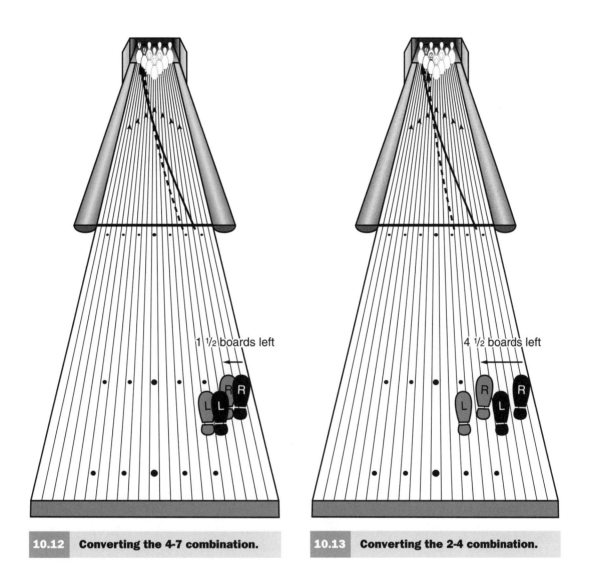

1 ½ boards left

4 ½ boards left

10.12 Converting the 4-7 combination.

10.13 Converting the 2-4 combination.

spare is to move six boards to the left, then the adjustment for the 2-4 spare is to move approximately 4.5 boards to the left.

Other 2-4 combinations that require the same adjustment include the 2-4-7 and the 2-7.

Hitting the Corner Pin

Many bowlers express concern over shooting the corner pin. Mental blocks, regardless of whether bowlers admit to having them, are not conducive to picking up this spare, nor do they develop confidence. Actually, the problem is rarely mental. Usually, the problem is physical, but it is blamed on the mental game. Frankly, it is easier to blame the mental game and accept the errors than to work at fixing the problem.

The corner pin should not cause problems if you shoot at it properly. Missing the corner pin is commonly caused by one of four things:

1. using a muscled arm swing that does not allow the ball to slide across the lane;
2. using an incorrect angle instead of angling the shot from the left side of the lane through the third or fourth arrows on the lane;
3. failing to open the shoulders while maintaining the proper angle at the foul line by walking straight from the stance position; or
4. using a ball that hooks past the spare because it is too aggressive to use at the corner pin.

The secret is to maintain enough angle to shoot cross-lane and to use the right ball to create less hook. Bowling balls today create a lot of friction with the lane and can hook strongly. When shooting a corner pin, such as the 10 pin, using a strike ball may make the shot more difficult unless you are proficient at altering the release to create less hook on a ball that is hooking too much. To get the ball to slide rather than hook, either change the release to a weaker wrist position or use a plastic ball that will hook less and slide toward the pin to convert the corner-pin spare. This is what the pros do to pick up this spare more consistently.

Establishing a consistent shot to convert the corner pin spare is the key to adjusting for all other spares on the right side of the lane. Walking straight (to maintain the optimal angle) while keeping the shoulders open will leave you feeling as if you are side-stepping to shoot the corner pin. But, once you get comfortable with the body position necessary to walk straight while maintaining open shoulders, you will maintain the optimal angle to shoot the 10 pin while aligning the swing with the target line to the pin. Picking up the corner pin will become routine!

Also, for the remaining right-side spares, bowlers often make the mistake of trying to adjust to the left from the strike line. Remember, for spares on the right side, begin to engineer your shot by identifying your target between the third and fourth arrows, move to the corner-pin position, and adjust by moving your feet from the corner-pin target line, not from the strike line.

CORNER PIN DRILL

Learn to walk straight and with open shoulders to convert the corner pin. Learn to start on approximately board 35, and walk straight to the end of board 35. Keep the target between the third and fourth arrows and angle the shoulders open to convert the spare.

To check your walk, use your slide foot to note the board you start on and the board you end on. Because there may be more dots at the beginning of the approach than at the end of the approach, you may not start on a dot in the stance on board 35, but you may end on a dot on board 35 at the foul line if you walk straight. Get used to counting boards, whether or not they have a dot on them on the approach.

To gain confidence, pick up three or more consecutive 10 pins, either from a full rack of pins or by pretending to shoot the corner pin that is not showing. The more disciplined you are in learning to pick up several corner pins in a row, the more confident you'll become. This is the way to overcome any mental or physical block in converting the corner pin.

MAKING A MARK

Play a game that emphasizes hitting the pocket and marking in each frame (getting a strike or a spare). Get a paper score sheet from the control counter in the bowling center. Keep score by hand. If you hit the pocket and strike, give yourself 2 points. If you hit the pocket and spare, give yourself 1 point. If you miss the pocket and strike or spare, give yourself 0 points. If you hit the pocket and miss the spare, subtract 1 point. If you miss the pocket and miss the spare, subtract 2 points. If you miss a single-pin spare, subtract 3 points.

The best possible score per frame is 2 points. The best possible score for 10 frames is 20. If you miss the pocket every frame and fail to mark, you score –20. If you hit the pocket each frame and miss every spare, you score –10. If you miss the pocket every time and still mark, you score 0. If you hit the pocket every frame and pick up every spare, you score 10. Strike every shot and you get a perfect 20.

Any positive score is good. This game emphasizes and rewards hitting the pocket and picking up spares. Don't miss those single pins; the error costs 3 points!

Next Frame

To shoot spares on the right side of the lane, start with the corner-pin shot. Start on the far-left side of the approach with your shoulders facing the target and pin, and walk straight to maintain this angle throughout the approach. The corner-pin shot serves as the point of reference for all other right-side spares.

Becoming skilled at the corner-pin shot is a matter of finding the correct angle, maintaining a relaxed swing, and using a ball that does not overreact. Bowlers who confess to having difficulty with this spare often allude to the mental game as the culprit. Often the mental game does not start out as the culprit. Poor angle, a muscled swing, and an overly aggressive ball are usually reasons for missing the corner-pin spare. If you make these mistakes enough to miss the corner-pin spare, then it really does becomes mental!

Open Bowling and League Play

Bowling for fun or practice is referred to as open bowling. The opportunity to open-bowl depends on lane availability outside league play. The cost of open play varies according to lane availability. Specials may be offered depending on the time of day. Open bowling is available when leagues are not occupying the lanes.

Many bowling centers offer organized leagues that you can join so that you can compete regularly on a recreational or competitive level. League play is mostly a social occasion for bowlers who enjoy the sport and enjoy being with one another.

Leagues offer various structures, including differences in duration, time, team size, and skill level. Different types of leagues use different scoring systems to manage the competition points and determine league standings from week to week. Dues include bowling fees and any sanction fee and may include additional money toward a prize fund that will be dispersed at the end of the league season according to the final standings of your team.

You can join a league as a team or you can ask to be placed onto a team for the season. Bowling centers run enough varied leagues to suit most bowlers. Inquire at your local bowling center about getting into a league. You may enjoy being on the team you join. Eventually you may form your own team with your friends or family.

League Play

Go to your local bowling center and find a league that fits you. The staff at the bowling center will help you find a league that will suit you. Playing with other bowlers of the same skill level will help you feel comfortable and have a good time as you develop your skills.

The length of league seasons vary; generally they range from 14 weeks to 36 weeks. Leagues are offered at various times on different days of the week. Most are held weekly but some are bimonthly (bowling every other week). Leagues are also popular on the weekends. Typically leagues are made up of teams of three, four, or five members per team.

The scoring system varies from league to league. There are women's leagues, men's leagues, youth leagues, mixed leagues, and seniors' leagues. The majority of leagues are handicapped leagues, but some are more competitive and based on your actual, or "scratch," score. In a handicapped league, you will receive a given amount of pins per game to add to your score, based on the difference between your average score and a standard score set forth by that league. In a scratch league, no pins are added to handicap your level of play.

Handicaps are based on your average. Your average is tabulated and updated every week. To calculate your average, divide the amount of games you bowl by your total score for those games. For example, if you bowl a 450 series (total score for 3 games), divide 450 by 3 to get an average score of 150 per game. In leagues, the secretary keeps track of the total pinfall for all games bowled and divides the total pinfall by the total number of games that have been bowled to keep each bowler's average updated, week to week.

Leagues compete on a schedule. Each team is assigned to a different lane each week. Teams that share a pair of lanes compete against each other that week. Bowlers complete a game, alternating frames on each of the two lanes. Competition points are kept according to the league rules, and the standings are updated each week.

A league secretary keeps track of the data for each bowler, each team, and the entire league. Each week, a standings sheet (figure 11.1) shows the current team standings, lane assignments of each

League Standings
Score Lanes

League #305: Taylor Classic
Week #34

Wednesday - 7:30 P.M.   Position   0% of diff - 4 Points
League President: Jerry Perna   Phone:
League Secretary: Craig Greenhill   Phone:
League Sanction Number: Results-Week 16 of 18 (35)

	Team Standings	Lane	Won	Lost	Pins	Won	Lost
1.	# 1-Tapemaster	25	47	17	90731	88	44
2.	#13-Motor City Electric	26	44	20	96514	85	47
3.	#7-Bowlers Aid Pro-Shop	27	38	26	93910	74.5	57.5
4.	#9-McCally Tool	28	36	28	97842	79	53
5.	#10-Lamoureux Custom	29	36	28	92755	70	62
6.	#11-Rustic Manor	30	34.5	29.5	96249	80	52
7.	#2-Muffler Man	15	34	30	96411	71	61
8.	#8-Legion of Doom	16	33.5	30.5	94260	74.5	57.5
9.	#14-Cigar & Gigg Van Born	17	33	31	90972	71.5	60.5
10.	#12-Pure Gold	18	33	31	87398	64.5	67.5
11.	#5-Jacks Painting	19	32	32	93738	64	68
12.	#6-North West Tool & Supply	20	30	34	84520	65	67
13.	#4-S W Coin Laundry	21	29	35	89439	60	72
14.	#3-Competition Graphics	22	27.5	36.5	89666	61.5	70.5
15.	#15-Good Times	23	18.5	45.5	76999	32.5	99.5
16.	#16-Team Sixteen	24	0	64	6910	0	132

Secretary on Lane 26

High Scr. Game	High Scr. Series	High Average
290 Gary Brandana	793 Brian Gwozdz	217.4 Bill Sennett Jr
290 Mark Tousignant	775 Bill Sennett Jr	212.0 Mark Lapshan
289 Len Grocki	764 Marty Knight	210.3 Todd Harbowy

High Scr. Game—Team	High Scr. Series—Team
1188 Muffler Man	3351 McCally Tool
1154 McCally Tool	3303 Rustic Manor

1ST	Last Week's High Scores	***2ND***
+133 Jerry Perna	Most Pins Over Average	+124 Dave Fox

High of the Night: $55   Mystery:
Tousignant 267   1. Mike Smith 180 $65
                                2. Kirk Mekdrum 195 $65

Split Made By:
Darrell Banks 7-10   Progressive:
                                292-Carry Over $252

                                Lucky Strike:
                                Carry Over $42

11.1   Sample standings sheet.

team, and a listing of averages for each bowler in the league, organized by teams.

You may join a league as a team or you can request to be put on a team in the league of your choice. Leagues do run all year round, but leagues are most abundant during the fall and winter. Late summer is a good time to inquire about fall and winter league openings. Late spring is a good time to inquire about shorter summer leagues.

Keeping Score

Although the league secretary keeps track of the standings and average, it's important for you to know how to keep score when you bowl. Most bowling centers have automatic scoring, but you need to understand how scores add up to realize the importance of your pin count in certain situations.

Score is based on a possible two balls per frame. A complete game is 10 frames. The first score is recorded in the upper frame. Use a number to reflect the number of pins knocked down; use a symbol to reflect a strike or spare. A strike (usually indicated by an X) is knocking down all 10 pins in one shot; a spare (usually indicated by a slash) is knocking down all 10 pins in two shots. The score is then added from frame to frame and recorded on the bottom of the frame. Figure 11.2 shows a sample score sheet.

Each frame is figured separately and added to the next frame to keep the score. The values for strikes and spares depend on the pin count on subsequent shots. Once you know how to keep score, you can appreciate how much a strike or spare can be worth depending on how many pins are knocked down on the next shots.

To determine the score for the frame, add the number of pins knocked down for that frame. Strikes are worth 10, plus the total pinfall for the next two shots; spares are worth 10, plus the total

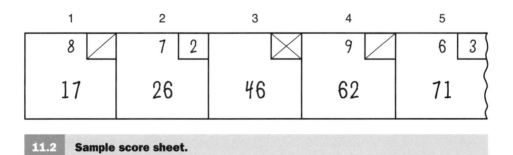

11.2 Sample score sheet.

pins on the next shot. So, if in the first frame you have 8 and then knock down the remaining 2 pins to spare, that gives you at least 10 for that frame, plus the amount knocked down on the next shot. If you get 7 on your first shot of the next frame, you will add 7 to the spare in the previous frame to score a total of 17 in the first frame. If you get 2 on the next shot, you will receive a total of 9 for the second frame, and add it to the score in the first frame, to have a score of 26 in the second frame. A strike on the next shot will be worth at least 10 in the third frame, depending on the total number of pins knocked down on the next two shots. If in the fourth frame you get 9 and spare, you will add a total of 10 more to the initial value of 10 for the strike, to get a total of 20 in the third frame. Added to the previous frame, that gives you a score of 46 in the third frame. The amount of the fourth frame will depend on the pinfall of the next shot. If in the fifth frame you get 6 and only pick up 3 more, you will add 6 to the spare in the fourth frame, for a total of 16, then add it to the previous total in the third frame. That gives you 62 in the fourth, and for the fifth frame add the total of 9 pins to the fourth frame total, for a score of 71 in the fifth.

During open bowling at the bowling center, practice keeping score. Most bowling centers will have paper score sheets at the control counter. These are either what they used before they installed automatic scoring or what they use when the technology fails. In either case, this old-fashioned method of tracking scores will enable you to compare your scoring to that of the automatic scorer. Compare your sheet to the automatic computer and detect any errors you may have made in your addition.

If your score is different from the automatic score, it may be the number of pins that you recorded for that frame. In that case, it was not your addition from frame to frame, but your recollection of how many pins you actually knocked down on that shot. It is between you and the automatic scorer to determine who was correct!

Once you finish bowling, calculate your average score for the session by adding up your total game score (add the total scores for all the games you bowled), then divide that total by the number of games you bowled. Sometimes, you can access this information on the automatic scoring computer.

If you came to open bowling to practice, you may have been busy working on your skills rather than trying to knock down pins. It is good to bowl to improve your skills without paying much attention to pinfall. Nevertheless, you still can do this average calculation just to learn how to determine your average. The scorer will work, regardless of your practice routine. If you are working on improving your skills and disregarding the pins, remember that this average calculation is just for practice. The average score you get may be significantly less than you are used to getting because you were not trying to knock down the pins.

Lane Etiquette

During league play or open play, so many lanes are occupied at one time that it requires rules of order as to who goes up to bowl at any given time. Bowlers who are next to each other on consecutive lanes should not bowl at the same time. You must observe lane courtesy so that everyone is able to keep a flow to league or open play. Courtesy also allows each bowler to focus on her shot. It is good bowling etiquette to look both ways before getting onto the approach so that you don't bowl at the same time as another bowler.

If two bowlers on consecutive lanes are ready to bowl at the same time, good etiquette dictates that the player to the right go first. You can assume this rule and let him go or simply signal that the coast is clear. Usually a nod, a hand gesture, or even a comment will do. Once you extend lane courtesy to the player on your right, he has the right to go or extend the courtesy back to you. The right to go is then yours. This courtesy allows everyone to bowl in turn with little distraction, and it keeps leagues running smoothly.

Also refrain from talking to a player once she steps onto the approach. Some players have a preshot routine that begins when they head toward the approach and pick up the ball. That is a good time to refrain from talking to them, because they are beginning to take their turn. Focus is a big part of bowling, as it is in all sports. As much as league bowling is a social occasion, each bowler needs to take uninterrupted time to focus on making a good shot.

During open bowling, when you practice your bowling skills, practice your bowling etiquette as well. Depending on how busy the center is, there may not be any bowlers directly to the right or left of you. If the center isn't very busy, bowlers a few lanes down may be distracting, but this is a good time to notice how courteous you are. You may find yourself extending courtesy if it comes naturally for you. It is not essential but it often happens among bowlers who notice each other while practicing, even when they are not on neighboring lanes.

The common practice is to let the bowler to your right go first. If that bowler waves you on, you have been given courtesy to go first.

Final Frame

Bowling has one advantage over other sports: Generations can bowl together. Whether you open-bowl for fun or decide to bowl in a league, bowling can be an individual or family sport. Socially, bowling has provided what most people need to get out and enjoy a sport and socialize with little concern about skill level. Handicapped scoring levels out the playing field; and bowlers of any age, skill level, or experience can bowl together comfortably and enjoy the game.

Bowling is a sport to enjoy with your family and friends. With bowling, you'll find that the more you know, the more there is to learn.

USA Bowling Coaching is an organization committed to providing coaching to bowlers of all skill levels. USA Bowling–certified coaches provide Bronze-, Silver-, and Gold-level coaching to all bowlers who strive to bowl better. Coaching is the key to achieving the next level of play. With good coaching, any bowler can improve.

About the Writer

Michelle Mullen won four national titles including one major as well as nine regional titles in the Professional Women's Bowling Association. She has coached bowlers of all skill levels for over 16 years, is certified as a USA Bowling GOLD coach, is co-owner of Your Bowling Coach with renowned pro bowler Aleta Sill, and is cofounder of Professional Bowling Instruction, Inc.

Mullen is a former Team USA coach and has authored many instructional columns in various publications including *Bowling Magazine* and *Asian Bowling Digest*. She is a member of Bowling Writers Association of America; National Women's Bowling Writers, Inc.; and Mid-America Bowling Writers.

Mullen lives in Dearborn, Michigan. You can contact her through her Web site at www.yourbowlingcoach.com.

Sports Fundamentals Series

Learning sports basics has never been more effective—or more fun—than with the new Sports Fundamentals Series. These books enable recreational athletes to engage in the activity quickly. Quick participation, not hours of reading, makes learning more fun and more effective.

Each chapter addresses a specific skill for that particular sport, leading the athlete through a simple, four-step sequence:

- *You Can Do It:* The skill is introduced with sequential instructions and accompanying photographs.

- *More to Choose and Use:* Variations and extensions of the primary skill are covered.

- *Take It to the Court/Field:* Readers learn how to apply the skill in competition.

- *Give It a Go:* These provide several direct experiences for gauging, developing, and honing the skill.

The writers of the Sports Fundamentals Series books are veteran instructors and coaches with extensive knowledge of their sport. They make learning and playing the sport more enjoyable for readers. And because the series covers a wide selection of sports, you can get up to speed quickly on any sport you want to play.

In addition to Bowling, the Sports Fundamentals Series will include:

- Soccer
- Basketball
- Golf
- Softball
- Weight Training
- Archery
- Tennis
- Volleyball
- Racquetball

HUMAN KINETICS
The Premier Publisher for Sports & Fitness
P.O. Box 5076, Champaign, IL 61825-5076
www.HumanKinetics.com

2335

To place your order, U.S. customers call

TOLL FREE 800-747-4457
Canada 800-465-7301
Australia (08) 8277 1555
New Zealand 0064 9 448 1207
Europe +44 (0) 113 255 5665